Pearson's Canal Co
Welsh Waters

Published by **Wayzgoose**, Tatenhill Common, Staffordshire DE13 9RS
website: www.jmpearson.co.uk email: enquiries@jmpearson.co.uk
Copyright: Michael Pearson Tenth edition 2016 ISBN 978 0 9928492 2 1

Affectionately dedicated to the memory of Mike Webb of Brewood

WAYZGOOSE

BENTE and Stein Ove, our Norwegian 'in-laws', must have been under the impression that Britain's inland waterways were predominantly subterranean or carried on lofty, vertigo-inducing aqueducts high above the surrounding countryside. It was an understandable illusion, for we had commenced our cruise from Chirk Marina, and whichever way we went we would quickly be encountering tunnels and aqueducts. They could not have experienced a more dramatic introduction to our canal system. It was as if the first piece of music they'd ever heard was the opening bars of Beethoven's 5th Symphony. And why not? It was a legitimate tactic. After all, our son's marriage to their lovely daughter had been celebrated on the shores of Hardanger Fjord, and the sparkling morning after, we had breakfasted on a balcony, savouring panoramic views of mountains and water. In essence, we needed to pull out all the stops if we were going to compete. Besides, we were enjoying a bit of a waterway renaissance ourselves, seeing it freshly through their eyes, and remembering what had beguiled us about the Llangollen Canal, a little matter of thirty-eight years previously.

It had lost none of its allure. Llangollen itself was en fete for - having not bothered to read our own guide - we hadn't forseen that it would be Eisteddfod week when we arrived. The town - as one wit could not resist putting it - was humming! Thankfully there were still one or two berths to be had in the mooring basin. We hastened to catch the last steam train of the afternoon, puffing up the Dee valley to Berwyn where we alighted, blindfolded Jackie to get her across the suspension bridge, and walked back along the towpath, twice encountering horse-drawn boats in the process. A Chinese children's choir serenaded us back into Llangollen.

We were nagged by doubts of being able to find a table for dinner. We needn't have been. The Corn Mill squeezed us in and treated us to one of the best repasts of our lives; food, service and ambience being of an

Lock-wheeling

exceptionally high quality given how busy it was.

Woken at first light, by a chorus of ducks keen to sustain the Eisteddfod's choral tradition, I left the boat quietly and climbed to the top of Castell Dinas Bran in the footsteps of George Borrow and H. V. Morton; though not, as yet Bill Bryson, unless anyone knows better. Gaining the summit at 5.20am, some lines of Thomas Traherne (you know, that 17th century metaphysical poet) obligingly entered my head: 'Certainly Adam in Paradise had not more sweet and curious apprehensions of the world than I'. Sheep were lolling in the ruins, the sun was rising over Cheshire's western brim, and the railway viaduct at Cefn Mawr was lit up like a gold bracelet. Closer at hand the Llangollen Canal and the River Dee rolled about the valley floor like lovers. Even the main roads were empty. Though I was about an hour and fifty years too late to witness the Chester to Barmouth mail train, steaming up the valley with the early English editions.

At eight o'clock we set sail for Ellesmere, not stopping until we reached there just after the shops had shut. It was a warm, mostly sunny day in July, and we were struck by the preponderance of hire boats. On many canals now, they are in a minority. I put this down to the evolution of a generation of hire boaters, sufficiently entranced by the inland waterways to make them an all consuming obsession. Whether this is sustainable remains to be seen. So it was good to see that some of the hire boat crews were young, and one hoped that boating would come to mean more to them than an agreeable means of progressing from pub to pub without transgressing the Highway Code. In the half century since British Waterways first published *Cruising on the Llangollen Canal*, the subject of that guide has contributed more to the local economy than it ever did in cargo carrying days. The Canal & River Trust's maintenance team was maintaining a tradition too. When we took on water at half past ten, they were still in the yard, conscientiously limbering up for the day's assorted tasks.

Shropshire
Union

Mike Webb Country

SHROPSHIRE UNION CANAL Autherley Junction 3mls/11k/1hr

B E the envy of your peers. Begin your holiday beside the sewage works of Wolverhampton. Things can only get better. And they do. Quite quickly as it happens, for the Shropshire Union turns its back on the filter beds, shrugs off the conversational gambits of Pendeford's housing estates, and strides out into open country, never looking back. The beauty, though, of canal travel, is the opportunity it provides to explore the unexplored, and Autherley Junction is not without its moments. Take, for example, Bridge 1, through which boaters from the Staffordshire & Worcestershire Canal must pass to enter the six inch stop lock which separates them from the Shropshire Union. It sets the tone for the confident engineering style of the Birmingham & Liverpool Junction Canal, the original name of Thomas Telford's thirty-nine mile route between Autherley and Nantwich. Napton Narrowboats' hire base currently occupies premises originally erected for the collection of tolls, the stabling of horses, and other ancillary waterway activities. Known pithily to working boatmen as 'Cut End', this was, until 1970, the dominion of Sam Lomas,

an engaging character who had started work on the canals in 1916. A born raconteur, one of his favourite stories concerned how he had reported for his first day of work on the eve of his fourteenth birthday and was told to "sit outside the office and watch the boats go by" because he couldn't legally start until he was actually fourteen: 'And', Sam would gleefully inform anyone prepared to listen, 'That's exactly what I've been doing ever since!' Hard now not to envy so onerous a responsibility. In 1958 he was awarded an MBE for 'meritorious service'.

Old photographs show 'The Shroppie' stretching bleakly away from 'Cut End' across a flat and empty tract of land towards a low and undistinguished horizon. This, however, is no longer the case, for where houses haven't been built, there are swards of open public space, 'landscaped' indiscriminately with trees and vegetation. 'Green is good' the planners will tell you, but not necessarily when the result is anonymous. From Bridge 2, Reapers Walk leads to a convenience store, an Indian takeaway, buses into Wolverhampton, and a surprising survival ... a 17th century dovecote, sole remnant of Barnhurst Farm, a sizeable property which had once belonged to wealthy wool merchants, but demolished in the 1970s to make way for the

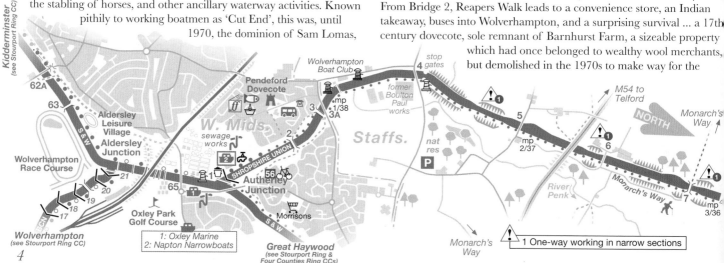

1: Oxley Marine
2: Napton Narrowboats

1 One-way working in narrow sections

4

housing estate.

Handsome cast iron mileposts measure distances between Autherley, Norbury and Nantwich, and by the time you reach the first of these the towpath has changed sides at Bridge 3, an elegant roving, or 'change-line' bridge, somewhat compromised now by the presence of the concrete latecomer beside it. Wolverhampton Boat Club built their premises here in 1966, having previously been eponymously based at Autherley; and, by all accounts, a very sociable club it is too. Sam Lomas was once their Commodore.

Industrial units east of the canal once belonged to the aircraft makers, Boulton Paul, builders of the not entirely successful WWII Defiant fighter plane. An aerodrome had been established between the Shropshire Union and Staffordshire & Worcestershire Canal in the 1930s. Amy Johnson flew demonstration flights from here in 1938. During the war a dummy factory

Avenue Bridge

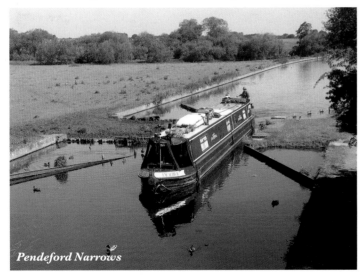

Pendeford Narrows

was erected a mile further up the canal, though there is no record of either works ever being attacked. Flippantly one imagines the enemy were happy for the dubious design to continue in production. To be on the safe side, stop gates were placed in the canal beyond Bridge 4, to minimise flooding were the canal to be breached.

An embankment carries the canal over the River Penk as a rural atmosphere is firmly established. A sequence of narrows and widenings ensues as the canal cuts through a band of Keuper Sandstone. Canalside cornfields are woven with a poppy trim. The M54, which links Telford to the M6, spans the canal, on a section completed in 1983. Briefly, the towpath is commandeered by the Monarch's Way, a 615 mile long approximation of King Charles II's convoluted escape route from Worcester to Brighton via Bristol and Yeovil in 1651. No motorways in those days.

GETTING into its characteristically loping stride, the old Birmingham & Liverpool Junction component of the Shropshire Union Canal forges north in a series of embankments and cuttings, known respectively as 'rockings' and 'valleys' to generations of working boatmen. As originally built - it was opened throughout in 1835 - its course across this agricultural landscape would have resembled an open wound. Long ago, however, absorbed into nature's rich tapestry, the canal now looks as if it has always been there, especially in this era of reduced maintenance regimes.

Having grown accustomed to the functional lines of Telford's overbridges, Bridge 10's ornamentation comes as a surprise. Known as Avenue Bridge, it was built to carry the carriageway to Chillington Hall. The advent of the canals heralded many similar attempts at ornamentation and disguise,

where powerful landowners would only condescend to permit a waterway to cross their parklands if suitable steps were taken to adorn the otherwise purely functional architecture of the new trade route. Chillington itself lies about a mile and a half to the west in grounds landscaped by Capability Brown. En route you encounter Giffard's Cross, where in the sixteenth century one of the Giffards (who have inhabited the estate for over eight hundred years) shot a marauding panther.

'Brood' is one of the prettiest villages on the Shropshire Union, if not the canal system as a whole. This is Mike Webb country: or perhaps that should be, 'Espionage Webb', as he was affectionately known on account of the meticulous records he kept of boat movements during the post-war years, when he was growing up in Brewood and attending the local

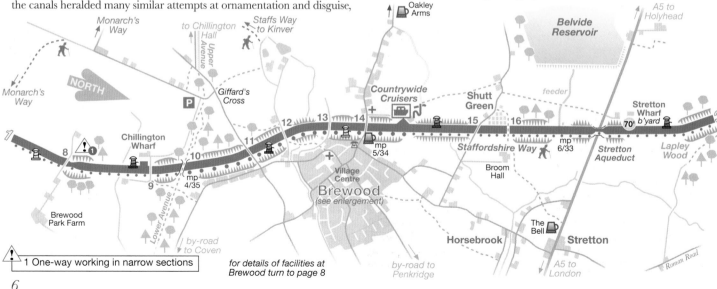

1 One-way working in narrow sections

for details of facilities at Brewood turn to page 8

grammar school, where he and his chums fell into the habit of collecting boat names because there was no nearby railway line at which to train-spot. But Mike's greatest legacy - painstakingly nutured by his widow Maria - is the vast number of photographs he took of working boats in the late 'fifties and early 'sixties, scarcely done justice in his slim volume *Shroppie Boats* published in 1985. Mike's funeral took place in Brewood in 2012. Fittingly his coffin arrived by boat. A bench just south of Bridge 14 commemorates this gentle soul together with a suitably illustrated memorial in the churchyard.

For two or three miles the towpath is made busier than usual by walkers doing the Staffordshire Way, a long distance footpath which seems to encounter a good many canals on its ninety mile wanderings between Kinver and Mow Cop. Belvide Reservoir is one of the main sources of water supply for the Shropshire Union Canal. It is also, under the auspices of the West Midland Bird Club, a magnet for ornithologists. Broom Hall, east of Bridge 16, was the home of William Carlos who hid King Charles II in the oak tree at nearby Boscobel after the Battle of Worcester in 1651.

Stretton Aqueduct

The canal crosses the old Roman Road of Watling Street on a sturdy, yet elegant aqueduct of iron, brick and stone construction. In his first attempt at guidebook compilation for *Waterways World* in 1981, the gnarled author of this guide erroneously drew attention to the intriguing juxtaposition at this point of Telford's Birmingham & Liverpool Junction Canal with his Holyhead Road. Happily, by the time he was publishing the first edition of this guide a year later, the truth had dawned on him that Telford had taken a short cut from Daventry to Oakengates, cutting out this section of Watling Street altogether. Memo to the Canal & River Trust; 'Stretton Aqueduct is long overdue a lick of paint'.

Boatbuilding and maintenance is undertaken at Stretton Wharf, beyond which the canal is once more engulfed by one of its trademark cuttings. Devotees of the *Canal Companions* - a secret society of extremely sagacious and good-looking personages - may care to learn that this very map was way back in 1981, the prototype from which all the maps in the series evolved. In its first guise it was hand drawn on cardboard, with a perspex flap for the second colour, and its lettering cut out and stuck on with gum; all a far cry from the Apple Mac which shoulders the work now.

Brewood

Map 2

Probably because it is so close to the county boundary, Brewood feels more like Shropshire; there being a 'west country' richness about it which comes as a surprise considering its proximity to Wolverhampton. Furthermore, there is a timelessness about 'Brood' which seduces you into spending longer here than you might have planned. Winding lanes of gracious houses lead to the old market place, enhancing one corner of which is 'Speedwell Castle', a Gothic fantasy erected in the 18th century on the winnings of a racehorse named Speedwell. The tall-spired parish church is notable for its Giffard family tombs. In the south-east side of the churchyard a stone backed by the carved image of a narrow boat pair commemorates Mike Webb, whilst elsewhere lies the grave of Hugh Rose, a Scots engineer who came here to build the canal. A plaque in the Market Place recalls that the engineering contractor, Thomas Andrew Walker, was born in Brewood in 1828. Among his achievements were the Manchester Ship Canal, Severn Tunnel and London's District Line. The Roman Catholic church, by Bridge 14, is the work of no less a Victorian architect than A. W. N. Pugin.

Eating & Drinking

BRIDGE INN - Bridge 14. Tel: 01902 903966. Much extended former boatmans' pub. Marston's & guest ales. Home cooked food. Open from noon. ST19 9BD
THE CURRY INN - Church Street. Tel: 01902 850989. Eat in or take-away Indian. Opens 5pm. ST19 9BT
LAZY DAYS - Stafford Street. Tel: 01902 850038. Pleasant little cafe open daily 9am-4pm. ST19 9DX
THE MESS - Market Place. Tel: 01902 851694. Daytime cafe and evening restaurant. ST19 9BS
THE OAKLEY ARMS - Kiddemore Green Road (1 mile west of Bridge 14). Tel: 01902 859800. Brunning

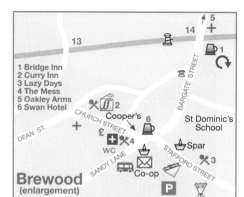

1 Bridge Inn
2 Curry Inn
3 Lazy Days
4 The Mess
5 Oakley Arms
6 Swan Hotel

Brewood
(enlargement)

& Price pub/restaurant housed in a former country club whose owner's twin daughters both married members of the rock group Deep Purple. ST19 9BQ
THE SWAN HOTEL - Market Place. Tel: 01902 850330. Cosy *Good Beer Guide* listed pub. ST19 9BS

Shopping

Spar (with cash machine), Co-op (inc post office) and branch of Lloyds Bank (9.30am-2.30pm, Mon, Tue, & Thur only). Cooper's foodstore is excellent, as is the Village Bakery for filled baps. Butchers W. Maiden & Son (Tel: 01902 850346 - ST19 9DX) are easily missed at the far end of Stafford Street. You can see pies being made on the premises and take away that Black Country delicacy, 'gray paes' or Staffordshire oatcakes.

Things to Do

CHILLINGTON HALL - about a mile and a half west of Bridge 10. Tel: 01902 850236. Guided tours on selected dates. WV8 1RE

Connections

BUSES - Select services 877/878 trundle back and forth between the market place and Wolverhampton

at roughly hourly intervals Mon-Sat, with some services continuing via Wheaton Aston to Stafford. Arriva 76A provides a limited Sunday service. Tel: 0871 200 2233.
TAXIS - Codsall Cars. Tel: 01902 846411.

Stretton

Map 2

Scattered village on and beside the Watling Street.

Eating & Drinking

THE BELL - Watling Street. Tel: 01902 850237. 'Noted Ham & Eggery'. ST19 9LN

Wheaton Aston

Map 3

Twinned with the sizeable town of Wheaton, Illinois, Wheaton Aston was once a small farming community but is now a peaceful suburban enclave.

Eating & Drinking

HARTLEY ARMS - Bridge 19. Tel: 01785 840232. Well-appointed canalside pub open from 11am. ST19 9NF
COACH & HORSES - High Street. Tel: 01785 841048. Village local which now does food (ex Tue). ST19 9NP
MOMTAJ SPICE - High Street. Tel: 01785 841381. Bangladeshi restaurant and take-away housed above the Coach & Horses. ST19 9NP

Shopping

The Lifestyle Express convenience store, with post office counter, is just three or four minutes away from the canal and opens 6am-9pm daily. Deeper into the village there's a small pharmacy and the Church Stores Spar which has an hour's lie-in but correspondingly stays open until 10pm - it does a nice line in hot snacks too. Turner's quaint canalside garage stocks Calor gas, diesel and boating accessories. Free range eggs from Bridge Farm close to Bridge 19.

Connections

BUSES - Select services 877/878 run approx half a dozen times Mon-Sat, to/from Wolverhampton (via Brewood) and Stafford. Tel: 0871 200 2233.

3 SHROPSHIRE UNION CANAL Wheaton Aston 4mls/1lk/1½hrs

NOTHING epitomises rural England quite so much as the ripe smell of muck-spreading, and there is plenty of opportunity to savour this fragrant bouquet as the canal traverses a landscape almost entirely given over to agriculture. Wheaton Aston Lock is of a solitary disposition, the only one in twenty-five miles of canal; a telling measure of Telford's advanced engineering techniques. Interestingly, as originally built, the locks on the B&LJ were equipped with mitred pairs of gates at both ends of each chamber.

The canal penetrates the deciduous heart of Lapley Wood, and there's another typically bosky Shroppie cutting by Little Onn, but elsewhere the embankments offer wide views eastwards towards Cannock Chase. How astonishingly remote and unpeopled the landscape seems. The West Midlands conurbation is less than a dozen miles to the south, yet moor for the night between Wheaton Aston and Little Onn, and you'll have only the occasional eerie hoot of a hunting owl, or the distant silent wash of headlights on a country lane, for company. Something of this sense of isolation must explain the survival of Mottey Meadows, alluvial flood meadowlands, unploughed for centuries, whose name apparently derives from the French word for peat - *motteux*. Sadly, though

perhaps understandably, access is by permit only, though there is an annual Haymaking Festival in late June at which time more of this fascinating landscape can be explored, encountering such rarities as the Horsetail Weevil and Snake's Head Fritillary, the latter at its most northerly location.

One of the canal's lengthy embankments carries it across a sequence of culverts which provide access between neighbouring fields. It also spans a brook which flows eastwards into the River Penk, registering the fact that this is the watershed between the Trent and the Severn. The ghost of a Roman Road bisects the canal at the southern end of Rye Hill Cutting.

Abandoned wartime aerodromes inevitably have their ghosts, and in decay accumulate a patina of lore and legend, hard to equate with the often mundane use to which they were put after closure. Wheaton Aston was opened in 1941 and became one of the RAF's largest training units, operating a squadron of 'Oxfords'. There were at least two canal dramas: once an American 'Thunderbolt' crash-landed in the waterway. Another well remembered wartime incident occurred at the lock when a narrowboat, carrying an unsheeted cargo of shining aluminium on a moonlit night, was attacked by a German aircraft which unleashed a bomb that exploded less than a hundred yards from the chamber. After the war the aerodrome's inhospitable huts were used for some twenty years as a transit depot for displaced persons, primarily Poles. Subsequently the site became a pig farm. Heartwarming, our British hospitality.

by-road to Bishops Wood

Coach & Horses
Momtaj Spice

Spar

Mottey Meadows (nat res)

Wheaton Aston

Hartley Arms 70'

school

Whitehouse Farm

Shushions Manor

aqueducts

by-road to Marston

resettlement site

Little Onn

St Edith's Well

Lapley Wood Cutting

18

17

mp 7/32

(S) Wheaton Aston Lock 7ft 0ins

19 mp 8/31

"Staffs Way" to Penkridge

(S) = WC

by-road to Penkridge

20

NORTH

20a

20b

20c mp 9/30

Roman Road

stop gate

21 22

former WWII aerodrome

Hall

23 mp 10/29 24

Rye Hill Cutting

by-road to Church Eaton

2

4

4 SHROPSHIRE UNION CANAL Gnosall 4½mls/0lks/2hrs

PERSISTING in its self-absorbed hike across the empty landscapes of west Staffordshire, The Shroppie even attempts to shun the little town of Gnosall, the name of which recalls to mind that old comic song by Flanders & Swann about The Gnu. In this case, you don't say Ger-no-sall, you say No-zull.

Near High Onn, the buildings of two wharves remain intact. One - now converted into a most desirable home - belonged to Cadbury's, the other to a local landowner, suggesting that there was once a degree of agricultural traffic on the canal. Logs, kindling and coal are on sale at the latter and winding permitted courtesy of the owner.

Deep shadowy sandstone cuttings, spanned - like leaping squirrels - by lichened red or grey stone bridges of simple balance and unaffected dignity, lead to the eighty-one unlined yards of Cowley Tunnel; the only one on the Shropshire Union. Cuttings such as this are apt to play aural and olfactory tricks on your senses. The blended aromas of bacon and diesel hang enticingly in the air and voices carry much further than you'd think: so be inclined to temper your remarks concerning the odd looking couple on that last boat you passed.

Curiously box-like, Bridge 35A used to carry a railway over the canal, but now forms the course of the Stafford & Newport Greenway, part of The Way For The Millennium, a forty mile long distance footpath connect-ing two extremities of Staffordshire, Newport to the west and Burton-on-Trent to the east. Historically, the railway was unusual in that it was actually built by the Shropshire Union Canal Company, apparently hedging their bets on the transport mode of the future. When, in 1846, they leased themselves to the London & North Western Railway, few shareholders would have backed the canal to outlast the railway. Now it forms a nice, traffic-free route for a jog before or after boating.

A couple of miles west of the canal at Bridge 37 lies Aqualate Mere which, at about a mile long, is the most extensive natural lake in the region. For its size it is remarkably shallow, having been scoured by retreating glaciers, and is notable in geological circles for its rare Esker deposits. Bitterns are regular visitors to its extensive reedbeds. Footpaths and bridleways provide access to the site which is managed as a National Nature Reserve by Natural England.

On a clear day the embankments north of Gnosall reveal that famous Shropshire landmark, The Wrekin, 15 miles to the south-west; a slumbering hunchback of a summit, 1335ft high.

A. E. Housman celebrated it in *A Shropshire Lad* - 'his forest fleece the Wrekin heaves' - and Salopians raise their glasses in a toast to: "All friends around the Wrekin".

[Map labels:] by-road to High Onn · former milk depot · Lord Talbot's Wharf · 70' · 26 · by-road to Bromstead Heath · by-road to Goosemoor · f'paths to Aqualate Mere · aq. · 3 · 25 · mp 11/28 · 27 · 28 · Royal Oak · Joan Eaton's Cross · by-road to Church Eaton · 29 · 30 · mp 12/27 · Chamberlain's Covert · by-road to Wood Eaton · Home Farm · 31 · 32 · Cowley Tunnel 81 yards · Gnosall Heath · Boat Inn · Royal Oak · Gnosall (csd 1964) · Co-op · Gnosall · A518 to Stafford · Way For The Millennium (course of Stafford-Shrewsbury railway) · A518 to Newport · The Navigation · mp 13/26 · 34 · 35 · 35 A · 36 · 37 · mp 14/25 · st · ga · NORTH

[Page number:] 10

Rye Hill Cutting

Church Eaton (Map 4)

Shopless village made remote by the huge tract of apparently empty countryside which characterises west Staffordshire. There's some Kempe glass in the church.

Eating & Drinking

ROYAL OAK - High Street (approx 15 mins walk east of Bridge 25). Tel: 01785 823078. Community-owned pub offering bar and restaurant food. Banks's, Marston's and local micro-brewery beers. ST20 0AJ

Gnosall Map 4

Gnosall Heath thrived with the coming of the canal and the railway not long afterwards, Gnosall stood back and watched with alarm, the onset of Progress. Two pubs slaked the thirst of passing boatmen, a steam powered flour mill took advantage of the new transport mode, and a non-conformist chapel kept a sense of proportion amidst all the excitement. Nowadays the pubs pander to pleasure boaters and passing motorists and the flour mill and chapel have become private residences. Half a mile east of the canal, Gnosall slumbers on its hilltop, the substantial parish church of St Lawrence (clerestoried nave and Norman pillars) being its most notable (though invariably locked) landmark.

Eating & Drinking

THE BOAT - Wharf Road (Bridge 34). Tel: 01785 822208. Marston's/Banks's pub with attractive curved wall abutting the bridge. Open from noon (5pm Mon), but shut between 2.30 and 5pm Tue-Fri. Congenially quiet in absence of TV, juke-box, gaming machines. ST20 0DA

THE NAVIGATION - Newport Road (Bridge 35). Tel: 01785 824562. Refurbished pub open from noon daily. Good choice of food. ST20 0BN.

ROYAL OAK - Newport Road. Tel: 01785 822362. Village local open from noon daily. ST20 0BL

Fish & chips on A518 open daily (except Sundays), both sessions. Tel: 01785 822806. No less than three take-aways: Bengal Spice (Tel: 01785 823248); Gnosall Chinese (Tel: 01785 823388); and Jia Jin Chinese/English (Tel: 01785 824388).

Shopping

Convenience store (with cash point) by Bridge 34. Another convenience store on way into Gnosall and Co-op in village itself, together with post office and Old Stacey's greengrocer/florist on High Street.

Connections

BUSES - Arriva service 5 half-hourly (hourly Sun) to/from Stafford and Telford. Tel: 0871 200 2233.

Norbury Junction Map 5

An atmospheric canal community, and although the suffix is misleading nowadays, Norbury remains a busy canal centre with a well equipped boatyard and a Canal & River Trust maintenance yard.

Eating & Drinking

OLD WHARF TEA ROOMS - canalside Bridge 38. All-day, all year licensed cafe; sizeable portions of homely cooking. Tel: 01785 284292. B&B and s/c accommodation also available. ST20 0PN

JUNCTION INN - canalside Bridge 38. Tel: 01785 284288. Open 'all day'. Food served lunch and evenings Mon-Fri; noon 'til nine Sat & Sun. ST20 0PN

Shopping

Excellent boatyard shop: provisions, off-licence, gifts, chandlery and a wide choice of canal books.

High Offley Map 5

ANCHOR INN - canalside Bridge 42. Tel: 01785 284569. Famously unspoilt *Good Beer Guide* listed boatman's pub which has been in the same family for generations. Devizes-brewed Wadworth 6X from the jug. Catering is restricted to sandwiches, but what delightfully innocent and simple sandwiches they are. Real pub, real ale, *real* treasure! ST20 0NB.

TALL trees disguise the immensity of Shelmore embankment and unfortunately curtail what would otherwise be panoramic views. Six years in the making it was, in its way, as glorious an engineering feat as any of Telford's more visibly imposing aqueducts. A veritable army of navvies and horses was employed on it. Spoil from the big cuttings at nearby Gnosall and Grub Street was brought by wagon for its construction. To Telford's dismay - conscious as he was that the bank need not have been tackled at all, had Lord Anson of Norbury Park sanctioned the preferred course through Shelmore Wood - the earthworks slipped time after time and, as the rest of the canal was finished, Shelmore stubbornly refused to hold. With Telford's health failing, an up and coming engineer called William Cubitt - who was to go on and make a name for himself as a railway builder - deputised. In March 1834 Telford paid his last visit to the canal, and Cubitt accompanied him on a conducted tour. Frail and deaf, the great engineer regarded the embankment which was the cause of so much delay and extra expense. One can picture the younger man confidently reassuring his elderly companion, but a few weeks after Telford's visit the bank slipped for the umpteenth time, and by the time Telford died, on 2nd September, his last canal remained uncompleted. Not until the following January was Shelmore Bank considered solid

enough for the canal to be put in water and for the first boat to gingerly proceed across.

Norbury is no longer a junction, though the name lives on, and a roving bridge spanning an arm which leads to a drydock at least sustains the illusion of another canal heading off into the unknown. The Newport Branch was abandoned by the LMS Railway in 1944, yet how nice it would be now to lock down its 'Seventeen Steps' and head across the marshy emptiness of Shropshire's Weald Moors to Shrewsbury. Exploration of the country roads west of the canal will reveal overbridges and the poignant remains of lock chambers. Vivid descriptions of the canal can be found in Jack Roberts' book of working boat memories.*

Staffordshire's Grub Street is not synonymous with the lower echelons of the literary trade ... though we often feel we have inhabited them for long enough ourselves. No, this Grub Street is known in canal circles as the location of another of the Shroppie's trademark cuttings. For over a mile the canal is wrapped in a thick coat of vegetation, again, like Shelmore, hiding the sheer size of the eighty foot deep cutting, whose most unusual feature is the double-arched bridge which carries the A519 across the canal.

The tiny telegraph pole is a survivor from the line which once marched beside the Shroppie. Appropriately, canals are again being used as lines of communication with the burying of optical fibres beneath selected lengths of towpath. A black, monkey-like creature is reputed to have haunted Bridge 39 ever since a boatman was killed here in the 19th century.

Shropshire Union Fly-Boats published by the Canal Book Shop, Audlem Mill

12

6 SHROPSHIRE UNION CANAL Shebdon & Knighton 4mls/0lks/1½hrs

CROSSING the border between Staffordshire and Shropshire, the canal continues to traverse an uncluttered countryside almost entirely given over to agriculture. A new crop conspicuous in neighbouring fields is elephant grass. It can come as a surprise to find so remote a landscape in the 'crowded' middle of England. One is tempted to categorise the area as 'lost' but for the obvious truth that it has never been 'found' in the first place.

Blithely we pleasure boaters sail across embankments and through cuttings with no more thought for their construction than if we were driving down the M6. But imagine the impact of Telford's brash new canal on the surrounding early nineteenth century landscape. Put yourself in the position of Sir Richard Whitworth's tenant farmer at Batchacre Park. Up until 1830 dawn rose across the open pasturelands throwing light through his east-facing windows. A year later his view of the rising sun was cut off forever by an embankment twice the height of the farmhouse. No wonder the landowners of this rural corner of Staffordshire had their misgivings, and the canal company paid dearly in compensation for the land they acquired. A series of leaks in the vicinity of Shebdon brought about closure of the canal in 2009, but thankfully soil-mixing techniques have now consolidated the bank.

West of the canal, there are good views of The Wrekin, with the Clee and Breidden hills prominent on the far horizon. You wouldn't expect to encounter a factory in the midst of otherwise empty countryside, but you do! It was opened by Cadbury, the chocolate manufacturers, in 1911 as a centre for processing milk collected from the dairy farming hinterland of the Shropshire Union Canal. Canal transport was used exclusively to bring countless churns gathered from numerous wharves along the canal; from simple wooden stages at the foot of fields, to the sophistication of Cadbury's own plant at High Onn. Cadbury owned a distinctive fleet of narrowboats, being one of the first operators to experiment with motorised craft. Cocoa and sugar crumb were also brought by boat to Knighton and blended with milk to make raw chocolate, itself returned to Bournville, again by boat, to be transformed into the finished delicacy. The last boatman to trade to Knighton was Charlie Atkins senior; eponymously nicknamed 'Chocolate Charlie'. He carried the final cargo from Knighton to Bournville in 1961, but some fine examples of historic craft are often to be seen moored here. These days the works trades under the name of Knighton Foods and produces dry powdered ingredients for drinks, desserts and baking products. Would that they were transported by narrowboat as opposed to juggernaut.

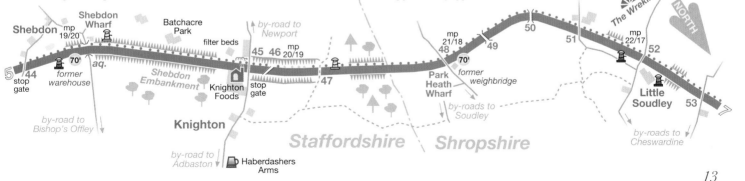

13

7 SHROPSHIRE UNION CANAL Goldstone & Tyrley 4mls/5lks/2hrs

THE Shroppie flirts with the county boundary as Staffordshire gives Shropshire a subtle dig in the ribs. The landscape, however, is impervious to the machinations of local government, remaining aloof and typically inscrutable: a tall, dark, silent canal, this Shropshire Union; much given, wittily, to brooding.

Woodseaves is another prodigious cutting: almost a hundred feet deep in places. These cuttings proved just as troublesome to Telford and his contractors as the embankments. In its raw, newly completed state, it must have corresponded to the canal at Corinth. Brittle at best, frequent rock falls were a fact of life. The Canal & River Trust, however, have to be congratulated on the remedial work they have undertaken in recent years, a happy by-product of which is that it is possible to walk the towpath through Woodseaves once again. Indeed, sufaced with granite chippings, and with the original coping stones revealed, the towpath must almost resemble that provided for horses when the canal was opened, though nature - as is her remorseless wont - is already fighting back. A feature of Woodseaves is its pair of high bridges, spanning the canal-like portals to the mysterious chasms of another world. They carry farm tracks and one is occasionally treated to a surreal encounter with a tractor passing loftily overhead, almost helicopter like in the context of the setting.

At Tyrley (pronounced 'Turley') a flight of five locks - the last to be faced southbound for seventeen miles - carries the canal down into, or up out of, Market Drayton. The lower chambers are located in a shadowy sandstone cutting across which branches intertwine to form a tunnel of trees. Damp, and rarely touched by sunlight, all manner of mosses and ferns flourish in this conducive environment. After dusk bats leave their tree bole roosts to hunt for insects, acrobatically twisting and turning over the luminous pounds between the locks. Fishing rights are under the auspices of Palethorpes Angling Society. We cheerily asked one angler if he'd caught anything: 'Not a sausage,' came the lugubrious reply.

Tyrley Wharf was a point of discharge and collection for the local estate at Peatswood; Cadburys also used to collect milk from here and take it by boat to their works at Knighton. The buildings date from 1841 and were erected in a graceful Tudor style by the local landowner. In the early 20th century northbound boats, tug-hauled up from Wolverhampton, would be taken forward by horse from this point, and extensive stabling was provided on either side of the canal. Nowadays, its commercial significance a thing of the dim and distant past, it would be difficult to imagine a more picturesque location, though those who remember Tyrley in the Eighties still miss the craft shop and home-baking outlet which briefly enlivened the scene here.

Goldstone Wharf mp 23/16 55 70' Wharf Tavern 56 mp 24/15 57 Woodseaves Cutting 58 54 NORTH Shropshire Staffordshire by-road to Cheswardine

Four Alls A529 Tyrley Grange mp 25/14 59 70' Tyrley Wharf 60 2 3 4 5 Tyrley Cutting Tyrley Locks 33ft 0ins 61 mp 26/13 Peatswood Estate R.Tern MD aqueduct

for details of facilities at Cheswardine and Tyrley turn to page 17

14

Bridge 67, Adderley

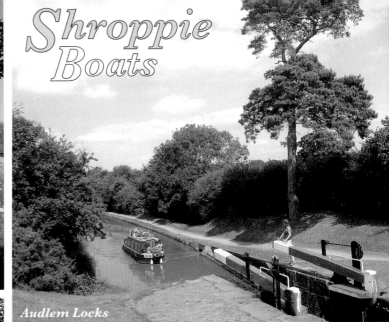

Shroppie Boats

Audlem Locks

Tyrley Locks

Bridge 104, Calveley

15

MARKET DRAYTON was the largest, in fact the *only*, town encountered by the old Birmingham & Liverpool Junction Canal on its route from Autherley to Nantwich. Naturally, a sizeable wharf was provided for dealing with local cargoes; though the canal's monopoly on local trade lasted only thirty years before the railway reached the town. It is sometimes difficult, in these days of the ubiquitous juggernaut, to appreciate the importance of the canal wharf and the railway goods yard to the past prosperity of small towns like 'Drayton. They must have been the hub of local life, few businesses would have been able to carry out their trade without regular recourse to the wharfinger and the stationmaster. From the opening of the canal until the First World War no commodity, apart from local agricultural produce, could have arrived at Market Drayton, or been dispatched, without the involvement of these important gentlemen. On the canal a large basin and a sizeable warehouse and adjoining cornmill remind us of this lost significance.

Pleasant 48 hour moorings, bordered by school playing fields, stretch south from Bridge 62 to the imposing aqueduct over the lane to Peatswood - Map 7. Steps lead down to the road below, which crosses the little River Tern nearby and forms the most romantic - but not perhaps the most convenient - approach to the town centre.

The canal makes a quick getaway north of 'Drayton. Note the substantial stone abutments where the North Staffordshire Railway once crossed the canal. The line opened in 1870 and closed in 1956. Passenger services to Stoke, sixteen miles to the east, were fairly sparse, but the railway threw off several profitable mineral branches.

Betton Cutting is not among 'The Shroppie's' most dramatic, but it is reputed to be haunted by a shrieking spectre, and working boatmen would avoid lingering here in the old days. Indeed, it could be said that this whole canal has something of a fey quality about it, a blurring of the homespun and outlandish which is liable to send shivers down susceptible spines.

The five locks of the Adderley flight limber you up for (or warm you down after) the fifteen of Audlem. In 1980 they ran to a resident lock-keeper - who went by the delightfully bucolic name of Frank Butter - and were so beautifully maintained and manicured that they won first prize in the National Lock & Bridge Competition. A privet hedge beside the third lock down indicates the site of a demolished lock-keeper's cottage, whilst a bench by Lock 4 commemorates canal stalwart Ike Argent.

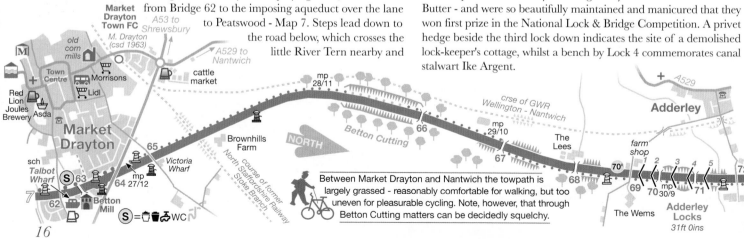

Between Market Drayton and Nantwich the towpath is largely grassed - reasonably comfortable for walking, but too uneven for pleasurable cycling. Note, however, that through Betton Cutting matters can be decidedly squelchy.

Cheswardine (Map 7)

Cheswardine lies a country mile to the east - say 25 minutes on foot - of the canal and can be accessed from bridges 52-55. High Street ascends to the parish church of St Swithin's much rebuilt by the Gothic Revival architect John Loughborough Pearson, best known for Truro Cathedral. 'Stately ... but not specially distinguished' was Pevsner's put down regarding the former. Now a care home, neo-Elizabethan Cheswardine Hall was erected in 1875 for the Newcastle-under-Lyme MP, Charles Donaldson-Hudson.

Eating & Drinking

THE WHARF TAVERN - Goldstone Wharf (Bridge 55). Tel: 01630 661226. A popular port of call throughout the boating season for good pub grub. Caravan and camp site, self-catering and spacious garden. TF9 2LP.
FOX & HOUNDS - High Street. Tel: 01630 661244. Joule's house - so the tasty beer (see column 2) doesn't have far to come. Food available lunchtimes and evenings Tue-Fri, and from noon Sat & Sun. TF9 2RS

Shopping

A delightful and welcoming community shop adjoins the Fox & Hounds. Open Mon-Fri 7.30am-10am and 3pm-5pm; Sat 9am-11am; Sun 9am-10.30am.

Tyrley   Map 7

Ten minutes west of Tyrley Wharf (past Tyrley's reticent little redbrick church) you'll come upon The Four Alls which offers breakfast, bar and restaurant meals and also accommodation Tel: 01630 652995 - TF9 2AG

Market Drayton   Map 8

The conspicuous Second World War pillbox guarding Bridge 62 does not, despite initial fears, remain in situ to repel visitors. Nevertheless, 'Drayton is best visited on a Wednesday when the ancient market is in full swing and country folk gather to seek out a bargain and a gossip. This is the town's real strength, along with its half-timbered houses which mostly date from the aftermath of a fire that swept through the place in 1651. Drayton's most famous son was Robert Clive, best remembered here for scaling the sturdy tower of St Mary's and for blackmailing local shopkeepers - ideal escapades in preparation for a career in diplomacy and military leadership. He established British rule in the Sub Continent and became known as 'Clive of India'. Betjeman and Piper's Shell Guide of 1951 recalls that the district was once terrorised by a murderous gang known as 'The Bravoes of Market Drayton'. On Saturday nights, as the pubs empty, it's easy to believe they are still at large. To the west of the town lie the large premises of Muller - 'the UK's most loved dairy product brand' - whilst on the northern fringe is 'Drayton's Livestock Market, a flourishing centre for agricultural buying and selling; excitable bidding can be heard, borne on the wind, as far out as the towpath.

Eating & Drinking

THE BUTTERCROSS - Cheshire Street. Tel: 01630 656510. Comfortable old fashioned tea room picturesquely situated alongside its namesake. TF9 1PF
CLIVE & COFFYNE - Shropshire Street. Tel: 01630 652272. *Good Beer Guide* listed pub dispensing Shropshire brewed Big Shed ales. TF9 3BY
JONES'S - High Street. Tel: 01630 652042. Well-appointed coffee shop open 9am to 4pm ex Sun and on Thur-Sat evenings from 6.30pm for pizzas etc. Sister establishment in Whitchurch - see page 46. TF9 1QB
NEW AMBROSIA - Cheshire Street. Tel: 01630 658382. Chinese, Asian & Thai cuisine to eat in or take-away from 5pm daily ex Mon. TF9 1PD
RED LION - Great Hales Street. Tel: 01630 652602. Joule's Brewery was originally in Stone but closed in 1974. The name, happily, was revived in 2010 and their beers are brewed here in Drayton using local mineral water. The Red Lion is the 'brewery tap' and a very fine establishment it is too. Open from 11am. TF9 1JP

Shopping

'It comes to something when even the charity shops are closing down' we overhead one local bemoaning, and it can't be easy for small market towns to compete these days, let alone small independent shops. Yet Market Drayton tries hard and looks its best on a Wednesday, market day. Drayton Deli is a good food shop beside the handsome Buttercross. Branches of all the main banks, a post office, launderette (though quite a hike from the canal - ask locally for directions) and Asda, Lidl and Morrisons supermarkets will cater adequately for most boaters' requirements.

Things to Do

MUSEUM - Shropshire Street. Tel: 01630 657455. Open Tue, Wed, Fri, & Sat mornings from April to October. Admission free. Local history nostalgically displayed in an old shop. TF9 3DA
SWIMMING CENTRE - Phoenix Bank. Tel: 01630 655177. Indoor and outdoor (May-Sep) pools. TF9 1JT

Connections

BUSES - service 64 operates hourly Mon-Sat, bi-hourly Sun to/from Shrewsbury to the west and Hanley (Stoke-on-Trent) via Newcastle-under-Lyme Tel: 0871 200 2233.
TAXIS - First Call Taxis. Tel: 01630 653200.

Adderley   Map 8

Scattered village forgetful of the fact that it once boasted a railway station. The isolated church largely dates from 1800 and is under the care of the Churches Conservation Trust. Lovely ironwork tracery on clear glass windows and a mounting block. At Lock 1 on the Adderley Flight stands Adderley Wharf Farm Shop run by a young couple called Simon and Alison. Free range eggs, home made cakes, lamb, pork and bacon are on sale. Tel: 0771 031 2747 or 0794 738 9098. TF9 3TN

17

RESPLENDENT in trademark 'Shroppie' grey and white paint, the Audlem flight is a pleasure: whether you are working up or down it, or simply spectating; and how often can you say that! Thirty-one miles out from Autherley, northbound travellers encounter Cheshire for the first time. Then fifteen locks, snuggled in a brackeny cutting of larch and Scots pine, drop the canal the best part of a hundred feet. Needless to say, the flight can be busy, and at such times patience, courtesy and good humour have their rewards. To paraphrase some old advice: be nice to people when you're working up lock flights, because you might meet the same people coming down. One or two of the lock chambers have retained their keeper's cottages, others have lost them, though at Lock 7 you can still smell the scents of garden flowers. Back in the present day, cakes and other morale-boosting edibles are often available at Kinsell Farm; ditto vegetables and fruit from an honesty box by Lock 9.

The barrel-roofed building by Lock 10 was used by stonemasons, blacksmiths and carpenters engaged in maintenance. Towards the foot of the flight - known to old boatmen as the Audlem "Thick" - you pass Audlem Wharf, one of the prettiest ports of call on the Shropshire Union, with a former warehouse restored as a popular pub and the adjacent lofty

Kingbur Mill converted into a superb craft shop. The mill was built during the First World War by H. Kingsley Burton, hence the name. It produced animal feeds; boats brought in raw materials and took away sacks of feed. Old photographs depict a covered gantry which spanned the roadway and jutted out over the canal to facilitate loading and unloading. The mill ceased working in the nineteen-sixties and was converted into a canal shop in the 'seventies by the late John Stothert, much of its internal fittings and machinery being atmospherically retained.

Shadowing the Shropshire Union - which belonged to the London & North Western Railway by the time the railway age was in full swing - the rival Great Western company's Wellington to Nantwich and Crewe route was a useful means of competition. The crane which adorns the wharf outside the Shroppie Fly pub belonged at the railway station before it was resited. Audlem station closed in 1963, but not before it had been immortalised by Flanders & Swann in their melancholy elegy to the Beeching axe, *Slow Train*. George Dow, the railway public relations officer, historian and early designer and advocate of diagrammatic maps, lived in Audlem for many years, his close friend Hamilton Ellis being a regular visitor. What a shame the latter wasn't cajoled into portraying the flight in one of his inimitable oil paintings, after

all it was in railway ownership for a century. Beside the bottom lock community allotments are nutured, then, passing a well preserved stable block - home to Pete and Jane Marshall of the Daystar Theatre Group - the canal, wide with concrete banking but deceptively shallow, bounds across the strippling River Weaver on a high embankment.

One of the crazier notions of the Ministry of War Transport during the Second World War was to make the Weaver navigable by 100 ton barges to this point, beyond which a lift would carry them up to the level of the Shropshire Union, upgraded sufficiently for them to travel as far south as Wolverhampton. OverWater is one of the new breed of 'farmland' marinas. A waterbus service links the marina with Audlem on summer weekends. Bridge 80 retains its early British Waterways era blue and yellow number plate, immediately to the south, a drainage paddle is embossed 'SUC Ellesmere 1928'; minor artefacts of enduring value.

Audlem
Map 9

Lovely old Audlem has grown in confidence and commerce in the forty odd years we've known it, and its annual Festival of Transport and Gathering of Historic Boats in July only serves to put it even more firmly on the map. Yet the village seems comfortable with its burgeoning popularity, and assimilates visitors without descending into self-conscious vulgarity. Canal apart, high points include the ancient buttermarket and parish church in photogenic juxtaposition.

Eating & Drinking
AUDLEM KEBAB HOUSE - Tel: 01270 812226. Shropshire Street.Open daily from 4pm for take-away: kebabs, burgers, chickens. CW3 0AE
THE BRIDGE - canalside Bridge 78. Tel: 01270 812928. Marston's, food daily 12pm-8pm. Nice etched windows pertaining to Marston & Thompson ... who remembers Thompson now? CW3 0DX
THE DELI - Shropshire Street. Tel: 01270 811554. Eat in or take-away bakery and coffee shop.CW3 0AH
JA'S - Cheshire Street. Tel: 01270 811488. Licensed coffee shop open daily ex Mon. CW3 0AH
THE LORD COMBERMERE - The Square. Tel: 01270 812277. Refurbished village centre pub. CW3 0AQ
THE OLD PRIEST HOUSE - The Square. Tel: 01270 811749. All day breakfasts, coffees, teas and light lunches. *Closed Tuesdays.* Fondly remembered as Mr Beaman's ice cream parlour. CW3 0AH

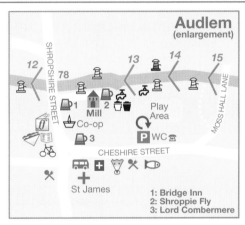

Audlem (enlargement)

Mill
Co-op
Play Area
P WC
CHESHIRE STREET
St James

1: Bridge Inn
2: Shroppie Fly
3: Lord Combermere

THE SHROPPIE FLY - canalside Lock 13. Tel: 01270 812379. Nicely furnished warehouse conversion serving bar and restaurant meals. Canalside seating. CW3 0DX
VILLAGE CHIPPY - Cheshire Street. Fish & chips. Tel: 01270 811777. CW3 0AH

Shopping
It's amazing to find a village with so many outlets. Indeed, shopping here is a pleasure rather than a stressful chore. Oxtail & Trotter's butchery (Tel: 01270 811793) on Cheshire Street is excellent, but there's also a well-stocked Co-op (ATM) open daily 7am-10pm, a Boots pharmacy, and a bicycle shop - Tel: 01270 811333 should you need running repairs. Laundry facilities at OverWater Marina by Bridge 80.

Things to Do
AUDLEM MILL CANAL SHOP - Tel: 01270 811059. Christine and Peter Silvester operate one of the best canal shops on the system and are congenial mines of local information to boot. As well as a wide range of gifts, crafts and needlework, the mill stocks an unrivalled range of canal books, and a growing list of self-published titles. Events are held throughout the year, and the mill celebrated its centenary in 2016. CW3 0DX
SECRET BUNKER - Hack Green, Map 10. Tel: 01270 629219. Open 10.30-5.30 daily during summer season - telephone for other times. Admission charge. Refreshments. "Experience a real four minute warning and view original TV broadcasts to be transmitted in event of a nuclear strike." Authentic equipment in its original macabre setting brings home the power of nuclear weapons and the government's state of readiness. Chilling stuff! CW5 8AQ

Connections
BUSES - service 73 to/from Nantwich roughly hourly and Whitchurch four times per day Mon-Sat. On Wednesdays service 75 provides a 'one-off' mid-morning link with Market Drayton, a boon for would-be towpath walkers. Tel: 0871 200 2233.

10 SHROPSHIRE UNION CANAL Hack Green 4mls/2lks/2hrs

GRUB Street, *Hack* Green: is the Shroppie scoring literary points? Itinerant canal writers apart, there are two isolated locks and the remnants of a stable at Hack Green, recalling the practice of frequent changing of horses on the 'fly' boats which travelled day and night with urgent, perishable cargoes, the sort of canal age equivalent of a lorry pull-in now.

This is the Cheshire Plain and dairy farming has long been a vital part of the area's economy - though for how much longer one might wonder, given the precarious state of agriculture in the 21st century. Making a profit from milk is notoriously difficult these days, no wonder farmers are being encouraged to replace cows with canal boats as demonstrated by a growing number of new marinas in the area.

When we first explored this canal in the early Eighties we were blissfully unaware of Hack Green's nuclear bunker, a Second World War radar station secretly designated to play a role as a Regional Government Headquarters in the event of a nuclear war. Deemed redundant at the end of the Cold War, it has somewhat bizarrely become a tourist attraction.

Adroitly changing the subject, let us recall how trade survived on this canal until the 1960s; which must be some sort of testimony to the viability of canal carrying. Perhaps in the final analysis attitudes rather than economics prevailed. One of the most celebrated traffics on the Shroppie in latter years was Thomas Clayton's oil run from Stanlow on the banks of the Mersey to Langley Green, near Oldbury in the Black Country. The contract commenced in 1924 and the Clayton boats, with their characteristic decked holds, and river names, were a mainstay of trade on the canal for thirty years. Even post-war, a thousand boat-loads per annum were being despatched from Stanlow, some remaining horse-drawn until the early Fifties. But, in common with other canals, the Shropshire Union lost its final freights to the motor lorry; then, for many, with the disappearance of its working boats, something died on the Shroppie, some intangible component of canal heritage that no amount of preservation, nor hectic holiday trade, can ever quite compensate for. On the outskirts of Nantwich the canal passes beneath the Crewe to Shrewsbury (and South Wales) railway line.

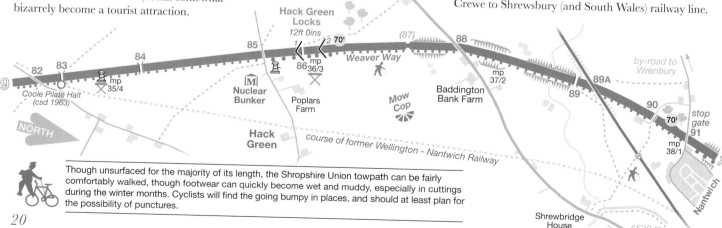

Though unsurfaced for the majority of its length, the Shropshire Union towpath can be fairly comfortably walked, though footwear can quickly become wet and muddy, especially in cuttings during the winter months. Cyclists will find the going bumpy in places, and should at least plan for the possibility of punctures.

11 SHROPSHIRE UNION Nantwich, Hurleston & Barbridge 5mls/0lks/2hrs

J UNCTIONS past and junctions present stimulate interest throughout this length of what has long been commonly known as the Shropshire Union Canal. The junction *past* lay at Nantwich, where Telford's narrow Birmingham & Liverpool Junction Canal - upon which work began at this end in 1827 - met the SUC's earlier constituent, the broad Chester Canal, opened as far as its terminal basin at Nantwich in 1779. The junctions *present* are at Hurleston - where the hugely popular Llangollen Canal commences its 44 mile, 21 lock journey into the mountainous heart of North Wales - and at Barbridge - where the Middlewich Branch of the Shropshire Union Canal provides a strategic link with the Trent & Mersey Canal. A broad embankment elevates the canal above the housing, back gardens and allotments which constitute the periphery of Nantwich. Ironically, these earthworks,

together with a cast iron aqueduct over the Chester road, could have been avoided if the owners of Dorfold Hall had not objected to the passage of the canal across their land. The aqueduct was refurbished in 2015. A Sculpture Trail has been laid out beside the embankment's refurbished towpath, the main exhibit being in the form of a boat horse built out of reclaimed lock gates. Nearby, stands a B&LJ milepost indicating that it's 39 miles to Autherley on the outskirts of Wolverhampton. Visitor moorings are provided along the length of the embankment, and they make for a pleasant overnight stay with easy access to the town centre, an enjoyable ten minutes stroll to the east.

The basin, former terminus of the Chester Canal, hints at the more expedient route to the south which Telford would have liked to have used; in the event it took him five years to complete the not strictly necessary earthworks. Nowadays the basin - still boasting a former cheese warehouse - is pretty choc-a-bloc with boats, all a far cry from 1939 when Tom and Angela Rolt couldn't get *Cressy* into the basin because a bar of silt, built up by the passage of motor boats, prevented their entry. Adjoining the basin are the premises of the Nantwich & Border Counties Yachting Club,

for details of facilities at Nantwich and Barbridge turn to page 23

21

Hotel Boats on Nantwich Embankment

Both junctions have suffered casualties in their infrastructure. There was a substantial junction house at Hurleston adjoining Bridge 97. Its dereliction (and subsequent demolition by British Waterways) so 'maddened' the financier, Sir John Smith (1923-2007), that he founded the Landmark Trust in 1962, a body dedicated to reviving old buildings for use as holiday homes. But perhaps even more regrettable was the loss in the 1950s of the warehouse and transhipment shed which spanned the main line at Barbridge, the sole remaining evidence of which is a narrowing in the canal to the south of the roving bridge over the Middlewich Branch.

At Wardle there's an old roadside 'pinfold' where stray cattle would have been penned. Nearby, the canal wriggles beneath Bridge 102 which carries the busy A51, a road that encounters a fair few canals on its desultory course between Tamworth and Chester. RAF Calveley was a shortlived Second World War training establishment.

Nantwich Aqueduct

an organisation whose founder members were early advocates of the use of the canal system for leisure.

The Leisure Age has impacted on the canal's agricultural hinterland as well. The Friesian milking herds which characterised these Cheshire pasturelands are not so prevalent now. Some farm buildings have been converted into domestic dwellings, other farm businesses, such as the Sadlers at Park Farm, have had to diversify, in this case into ice cream. You could say farming is not quite as black and white as it once was, more chocolate and vanilla.

Hurleston and Barbridge are the 'Clapham Junctions' of the inland waterways. At the height of the cruising season the section between them is often frenetic with boats converging from and diverging to all points of the canal compass. Lucky, then, that the old Chester Canal was built for use by 14ft beam barges known as 'Mersey Flats' and that there is plenty of room to manoeuvre.

Nantwich Map 11

North or south, there are few English towns of this size nicer than Nantwich. The octagonal tower of St Mary's church, glimpsed across freshly-built rooftops from the high canal embankment, tempts you to moor and get to know Nantwich better. Walking in from the basin, the aqueduct forms an appropriate portcullis, and the appeal of the town increases as the centre is reached. Welsh Row is a handsome thoroughfare: keep your eyes peeled for the Tollemache Almshouses, Cheshire Constabulary police houses, Primitive Methodist chapel and Town Well House (No.52). In medieval times Nantwich was the chief salt producing town in the county.

Eating & Drinking

AUSTINS - Hospital Street. Tel: 01270 625491. Consciously old fashioned coffee house which transcends kitsch by virtue of its range of comfort food including their very own bangers and mash, cottage pie, omelettes, cakes. Open Tue, Thur, Fri & Sat 10am to 3.30pm; Wed 10am to noon. CW5 5RL

BLACK LION - Welsh Row. Tel: 01270 628711. *Good Beer Guide* recommended 17th century half-timbered pub on way into town. Weetwood ales from nearby Tarporley. CW5 5ED

CAFE DE PARIS - Hospital Street. Tel: 01270 620180. Charming oasis of an establishment run, not by a Parisian, but by a gentleman from Orleans. Coffees, soups, baguettes, French pastries and light lunches. CW5 5RP

WATERSIDE CAFE - Nantwich Basin. Tel: 01270 626171. Breakfasts, coffees, lunches and teas. CW5 8LB

ROMAZZINO - Love Lane (off Pillory Street). Tel: 01270 626456. Well appointed Italian restaurant open for lunch and dinner daily. CW5 5BH

STREET - Welsh Row. Tel: 01270 625539. Open daily from noon for eat in or take-away burgers, burritos, noodles & curries: i.e. 'street food'. CW5 5ED

Shopping

Nantwich's antique shops and boutiques emphasise its position at the centre of a Gucci-heeled hinterland. Keep a tight rein on your womenfolk, without firm male guidance they will run amok in the town's fine clothes, shoes, and household goods outlets. But it is the food sellers that are most satisfying: butchers like Clewlows (in our top six canal-connected purveyors of pork pies), bakers like Chatwins (whose headquarters are in the town) and fishmongers like Sea Breezes all of whom have outlets in Pepper Street. On Hospital Street are A. T. Welch's surprisingly narrow yet deep premises housing butcher, grocer, delicatessen and coffee merchant counters. The indoor market hall is open on Tuesdays, Thursdays and Saturdays.

Laundry facilities are available at the canal basin, as are souvenirs and limited groceries from Julie & Garry's friendly little 'Shop on the Canal'.

Things to Do

TOURIST INFORMATION - Civic Hall. Tel: 01270 303150 or 628633. CW5 5DG

NANTWICH MUSEUM - Pillory Street. Tel: 01270 627104. Well presented displays of local history. Free admission. Small gift shop. CW5 5BQ

Connections

BUSES - Arriva service 84 connects quarter-hourly Mon-Sat (hourly Sun) with Crewe in one direction and hourly with Chester in the other, with useful stops at Barbridge and Calveley for towpath walkers. Tel: 0871 200 2233.

TRAINS - services to/from Crewe and Shrewsbury via Wrenbury and Whitchurch. Tel: 03457 484950.

TAXIS - Direct. Tel: 01270 585000.

Acton Map 11

A short walk across the fields from Bridge 93 leads to this village whose imposing church repays investigation, for amongst the gravestones you'll come upon that of A. N. Hornby, the English cricket captain whose one-off defeat to Australia at The Oval in 1882 brought about a spoof obituary which referred to the cremated 'remains' of the English game being sent to Australia, hence the origin of 'The Ashes'.

Barbridge Map 11

Eating & Drinking

OLDE BARBRIDGE INN - Old Chester Road (adjacent Bridge 100). Tel: 01270 528327. Canalside pub owned by the Woodlands Brewery. Open daily for food and drink from noon. CW5 6AY

Connections

BUSES - Arriva service 84 as Nantwich.

REMOTE, and seemingly always windswept, the Middlewich Branch of the Shropshire Union cuts across the grain of the landscape on a series of high embankments. It can be a busy length of canal for, as well as Four Counties Ring traffic, it funnels boats to and from the hugely popular Llangollen Canal, and there are two marinas on it as well. Consequently its four deep and heavy-gated locks can become bottlenecks at the beginning and end of summer weeks.

Historically, the branch, opened in 1833, belonged to the Chester Canal Company and was engineered by Thomas Telford. Trade was heavy in cargo-carrying days, as after opening of the Birmingham & Liverpool Junction Canal this became the optimum route between the Black Country and the industrial North-west. Traffic also developed between Ellesmere Port on the banks of the Mersey and The Potteries: Cornish china clay in one direction, finished crockery in the other.

At Cholmondeston the Crewe to Chester railway line, part of the historic route of the Irish Mails to Holyhead, crosses the canal. A high wooded embankment carries the canal across the River Weaver which rises on the south-facing slopes of the Peckforton Hills and passes beneath the Llangollen Canal at Wrenbury prior to becoming navigable at Winsford, less than five miles downstream of the Weaver Aqueduct.

Church Minshull - all russet coloured brick and black & white half timbering - looks, from the canal's elevated position, like a toy village embracing the river's luxuriant banks. Tom and Angela Rolt enjoyed an extended stay here in the fateful Autumn of 1939 while Tom worked for Rolls Royce at Crewe. It was tedious work he didn't enjoy, but the couple revelled in the close-knit community which flourished at Minshull: the blacksmith who shod the local cart horses; and the miller whose water wheels supplied the village with its electricity, continuing to do so right up until 1960.

Summary of Facilities

The Badger Inn at Church Minshull (Tel: 01270 522348 - CW5 6DY) is a smartly refurbished country inn (easily reached from Bridge 14) offering food and accommodation and open from 11.30am daily (noon Sun). There are cafes at both marinas, Aqueduct's The Galley being particularly good. Arriva bus service 31A operates hourly Mon-Sat from Church Minshull to Crewe. Tel: 0871 200 2233.

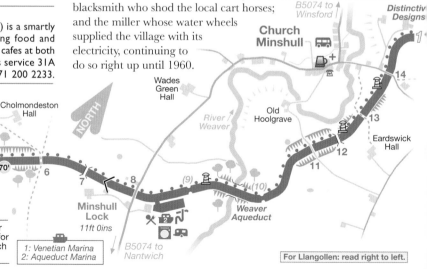

The Middlewich Branch's towpath is largely grassy: fine for well-shod walkers but horribly bumpy and uncomfortable for cycling until it reaches Clive Green (Map 11B), east of which it has been upgraded as part of National Cycleway No.5.

1: Venetian Marina
2: Aqueduct Marina

For Llangollen: read right to left.

TO subconsciously relegate the Middlewich Branch to the back of your mind as an unspectacular, but necessary link in the waterways of the North-West would be unjust, for this is a rumbustious canal, extrovertly ushering you loftily above the snaking valley of the Weaver, presenting you with expansive views towards a horizon bounded by Delamere Forest and the Peckforton Hills.

Several sizeable farms border the canal, their fields filled with dairy herds or cut red by the plough in a ruddy shade of corduroy. Some interesting old canal horse stables have been converted into living quarters by Bridge 18. Near Bridge 22, woods partially obscure the Top Flash, a subsidence induced lake beside the Weaver. The main London-Glasgow railway crosses the canal, its sleek electric trains swishing by at forty times the speed of your boat. To the south-east lies a forgotten, older transport route, a Roman road which linked the early salt mines at Nantwich and Middlewich.

Shaken out of its default setting torpor by the increasingly popular Folk & Boat Festival held each June, Middlewich embraces the Clog Dancing affinity between those who owe eternal gratitude to Cecil Sharp and Ralph Vaughan Williams, and those who are similarly indebted to Tom Rolt and Robert Aickman; indeed, in some cases their heroes are interchangeable. Throughout the rest of the year, Middlewich muddles through, sombrely reflecting on its saltier past when Seddons and Cerebos were at their zenith and a forest of flaring chimney stacks supported the gauzy sky. Further details of Middlewich and its facilities are to be found in Pearson's *Four Counties Ring* and *Cheshire Ring* Canal Companions. But here we must forsake its eponymous canal branch and head back to the main line at Barbridge.

Top Flash

Clive Green

5

Yew Tree Farm

Middlewich

Town Centre

172

22A

23 24 25

Park Farm

Wardle Lock

74-72

31

169

drydock

3

River Weaver

22

Dairy House

26

NORTH

21

Lea Hall

Stanthorne Lock
11ft 1in

27

Morrisons

Lidl

Twelve Acres

Weaver Bank

20

West Coast Main Line

A530

aqs.

Middle-wich

old stables

19

Tesco

70'

1A

15

16

70' (17)

18

Wimboldsley Hall

28

172

Minshull Vernon
(closed - 1942)

River Wheelock

29

30

31

Wardle Lock
9ft 9ins

M'wich Locks
74-72
32ft 7ins

For Llangollen: read right to left.

1: Andersen Boats
2: Middlewich Narrowboats
3: Kings Lock Chandlery

Kings Lock
11ft 3ins

Hardings Wood
(see Four Counties or Cheshire Ring CCs)

Preston Brook
(see Four Counties or Cheshire Ring CCs)

25

12 SHROPSHIRE UNION CANAL Bunbury & Beeston 4mls/5lks/2hrs

ONCE it has escaped the cacophony of the A51 at Calveley, this becomes an intoxicating length of waterway, full of contrasts in landscape: the wooded defile at Tilstone Bank; the glorious line of close-cropped hills running north of the two Beeston locks; and most dramatic of all for travellers heading northwards, the first detailed views of Beeston Castle, over five hundred feet high on its lonely outcrop. Through all this the little River Gowy chuckles to its Mersey outfall, draining the rolling farmland. But, scintillating scenery apart, it bears remembering that the old Chester Canal had a living to earn, and throughout this section there are well preserved examples of former commerce, notably the former transhipment wharf between canal and railway at Calveley, now employed by the Canal & River Trust as a 'Service Station'.

Bunbury is a fascinating canal environment. The wide-beam staircase locks make an obvious centrepiece. Alongside them is a fine stable block, recalling the practice of exchanging fresh horses for tired ones on the fast 'fly boats' which covered the 80 miles between the Mersey ports and the Black Country factories in just

over 24 hours. These premises are now occupied by Anglo Welsh, their offices and shop being accommodated in an adjacent warehouse still displaying the faded legend 'Shropshire Union Railways & Canal Co' on its north facing gable end. Tilstone Lock lies in a gorgeous setting. Beside it a former mill stands astride the Gowy, dating from 1838 and restored for residential use. A curious circular building overlooks the head of the lock chamber. There are others at Beeston and Tarvin locks and they were once used by lengthsmen to store maintenance equipment. This one has been admirably restored by the Chester Canal Heritage Trust. Beneath a sweeping ridge - reminiscent of the Kennet & Avon's progress beside the Berkshire Downs - the canal approaches the two Beeston locks, and in doing so crosses the Vyrnwy Aqueduct, a 68 mile pipeline constructed

Nag's Head

Dysart Arms
Bunbury

M Bunbury Mill

Bowe's Gate

Wild Boar

A49

Auction Mart

Beeston Castle Wharf

107

12 70'

11 Tiverton

River Gowy

105 15/14 70'

106

spw mill

13 Tilstone Bank

Clay's Farm

104

11

103 Countrywide 103A

J. S. Bailey Calveley coal merchant

Barrets Green Alpraham

Southley Farm

A51

NORTH

S

Locks
15 & 14 Bunbury Staircase Locks 15ft 7ins
13 Tilstone Lock 9ft 8ins
12 Beeston Stone Lock 8ft 6ins
11 Beeston Iron Lock 7ft 0ins

Tollemache Arms

S = WC

1: Anglo Welsh
2: Chas. Hardern

1: Calveley - csd 1960
2: Beeston Castle & Tarporley - csd 1966

in the 1880s from a dam in mid-Wales to Liverpool - see also Map 23. As originally built, the locks at Beeston formed a two chambered staircase on an alignment slightly to the north. Instabilities in the quicksand upon which it stood, however, brought about its collapse a dozen years after the canal was opened. Lacking sufficient capital to effect a repair, the canal remained effectively severed, goods being inconveniently transhipped along a tramway in the interim. Unsuccessful attempts were made to find a solution to the problem before Thomas Telford was consulted in 1827. He recommended replacement of the staircase by two single chambers, the lower being constructed of iron plates. An effective solution, proven by time, but the ground didn't give up easily, and down the years the chamber has become distorted, precluding its use by two narrowboats simultaneously, a restriction liberally signposted.

Beeston Castle Wharf doesn't lack interest. The cattle mart repays investigation, Friday being the regular day for livestock auctions, with machinery sales on selected dates as well. Deer graze on the hillside which conceals Second World War oil storage tanks. A charming old signal box perches on the railway embankment, still bearing the closed station's appellation - Beeston Castle & Tarporley. Chas. Hardern's boatyard is centered on a whitewashed building which originally provided stabling for boat horses, complete with first floor hay loft. The house by the bridge on the towpath side was formerly the Railway & Canal Inn.

Calveley   Map 12
Eating & Drinking/Shopping
J. S. BAILEY - Nantwich Road. Tel: 01829 262900. Suppliers of cheese to the catering industry, Bailey's run a shop and cafe at their Calveley Mill premises open from 8am to 5pm Mon-Fri and 8.30am to 4pm Sat. In addition to a wide range of cheese, the shop deals in everyday essentials (such as wine and beer), whilst the cafe (which is open *daily*) does breakfasts and daily specials along with lighter fare. CW6 9JW
Connections
BUSES - Arriva service 84 operates hourly, daily to/from Nantwich and Chester. Tel: 0871 200 2233.

Alpraham   Map 12
Eating & Drinking
TOLLEMACHE ARMS - Chester Road. Tel: 01829 261716. Well appointed pub/restaurant open all day and offering accommodation. CW6 9JE

Bunbury   Map 12
Masquerading as 'Great Paxford' in ITV's Second World War drama *Home Fires*, Bunbury suffered in wartime for real when the Luftwaffe, returning from a raid on Liverpool, jettisoned bombs, destroying several houses and damaging the parish church of St Boniface. One of Cheshire's finest churches, it contains many notable effigies and tombs.
Eating & Drinking
DYSART ARMS - Bowe's Gate Road. Tel: 01829 260183. Inimitable Brunning & Price country inn open from noon daily; well worth the walk! CW9 9PH *Fish & Chips in village centre open 11.30am-1.30pm and 5-8pm Tuesdays to Saturdays. Try also Tilly's Coffee Shop.*
Shopping
Well stocked Co-op convenience store with post office counter in the centre of the village about 20 minutes walk from the canal at bridges 105 or 106.
Things to Do
BUNBURY MILL - Bowe's Gate Road. Tel: 01829 260497. Open Sunday & Bank Hol Mon afternoons 1-5pm, April to October. Enchanting watermill with additional delight of a tearoom. CW9 9PY

Beeston   Maps 12 & 13
Eating & Drinking
SHADY OAK - Bate's Mill Lane (canalside Bridge 109). Tel: 01829 730718. Open from noon daily. CW6 9UE
Things to Do
BEESTON CASTLE - Chapel Lane (one mile south of Wharton's Lock along the Sandstone Trail). Tel: 01829 260464. Open daily under the aegis of English Heritage: 10am-6pm summer, 10am-4pm winter. Admission charge. Captured at least three times during its turbulent history - by Simon de Montfort in his revolt against Henry III, and by both the Roundheads and Cavaliers during the Civil War - this 13th century fortress commands a wonderful panorama from its upper keep, the canal being discernible all the way to Egg Bridge. CW6 9TX

Tattenhall   Map 13
Things to Do
ICE CREAM FARM - Newton Lane. Tel: 01829 770995. Huge family orientated visitor attraction offering indoor and outdoor activities, not to mention fifty flavours of ice cream made by the Fell family on site. Open daily 10am-5.30pm. Half a million people (annually) can't be wrong! CH3 9NE
Connections
BUSES - service 41A runs to/from Chester daily approximately bi-hourly. Tel: 0871 200 2233.

13 SHROPSHIRE UNION CANAL Beeston Castle 4mls/11k/2hrs

BEESTON Castle (which appeared on the Chester Canal Company's seal) dominates the landscape, like a visitor from another planet, an upturned plum pudding of an outcrop, a geological afterthought commandeered by medieval man for a fortress. Behind it the Peckforton Hills ride the horizon like surfers on an Atlantic beach. This is good hiking country. The Sandstone Trail, a 34 mile footpath across Cheshire's backbone from Frodsham to Whitchurch (see Map 19), crosses the canal at Wharton's Lock and may be conveniently linked with the towpath and other public footpaths to form a number of circular walks. Actually, Beeston isn't the only 'medieval' castle on view. Behind it stands Peckforton Castle, a Victorian gothic interloper used these days as a venue for weddings and corporate events. Incidentally, the lock-keeper's cottage at Wharton's Lock was destroyed by a stray German bomb during the Second World War, perhaps on the same occasion as Bunbury village was bombed. This, together with other illuminating facts, was gleaned from the Chester Canal Trust's excellent 2005 book *The Old Chester Canal*, edited and published on their behalf by Gordon Emery,

and a model of local canal history interpretation.

By Bridge 109, Bate's Mill survives as an enviable private residence; still, apparently employing water power as a source of electricity. A country road swoops down to cross the millstream and an adjacent expanse of water is the haunt of wildfowl. Beyond Bridge 111 the canal is carried over the Gowy on an embankment framed with larch trees. A public footpath passes through a culvert beneath the embankment. Trains rattle and hum across the middle distance, but otherwise the world seems undisturbed, and in the long pound between Wharton's and Christleton locks the boater has time for reflection and communing with nature.

A large marina adds considerably to boat movements in the vicinity and contrasts in approach to the lengthy linear moorings to be found on the following map. Various commercial enterprises cluster beside Crows Nest Bridge, No.113, but in times gone by there was a brick works and a bone mill here, the latter notorious for its evil-smelling processing of animal bones into glue and other by-products; though at least it brought traffic to the canal: coal in to fire its boilers, and finished products out.

Between Barbridge (Map 11) and Egg Bridge (Map 14) the towpath is clear though unsurfaced: fine for walkers in stout footwear, but far too bumpy for enjoyable cycling. From Egg Bridge down into Chester the towpath is metalled and a designated cycleway.

ALTHOUGH the countryside is conspicuously flat the Peckforton Hills to the south and Delamere Forest to the north-east give your gaze something to linger over; whilst, if the elements have blessed you with a clear day, the brooding summits of Celtic Wales are to be discerned on the western rim of the world. Long lines of moored craft make the considerate boater's progress irritatingly slow in the vicinity of Hargrave. As they approach Bridge 115, motorists honk their horns like excitable Mediterraneans at a fiesta.

Probably the very earliest hire cruisers on the canal system were available from a boatyard at Christleton which began hiring to intrepid holidaymakers way back in 1935. In those days you could hire a small cruiser for £4 a week, though you also had to fork out ten shillings in tolls to the LMS Railway who owned the canal prior to Nationalisation in 1947. In the 1920s, a Chester man, T. W. Cubbon, wrote an account (*Only a Little Cockboat*) of a voyage, in a canvas covered boat powered by a petrol engine, from Chester along the Shropshire Union and Staffs & Worcs canals to the rivers Severn and Avon. In the book he relates his first night

on the canal at Egg Bridge moored abreast a widebeam barge, but being forced to move on in the small hours of the morning because rats from the barge had boarded his boat. The barges and the rats may have gone, but signs of former commerce remain at Egg Bridge and Christleton in the form of handsome canalside mills. The curious, cast iron columned, hexagonal timber topped structure on the A41 is an old hydraulic sewage lift, manufactured by Adams of York circa 1900. At Christleton (a pleasant village with a Victorian church by Butterfield) the canal commences its descent to Chester and the surface of the towpath is laudably well maintained, all the way to Ellesmere Port.

Waverton

Quaint estate village with handsome sandstone church. At Common Farm is the Spitting Feathers Brewery whose output can be sampled at the Brewery Tap in Chester - see page 34.

Egg Bridge

Egg Bridge offers useful facilities both sides of Bridge 119. They include a post office stores (south-west); 'One Stop' convenience store (with cash machine), a deli/sandwich bar, pharmacy, and Pizza Guy (Tel: 01244 336006) which does baguettes, pizzas, kebabs and fish & chips. CH3 7NB

Christleton

CHESHIRE CAT - canalside between bridges 120 and 121. Tel: 01244 332200. 'Inn Keeping with Tradition' restaurant/pub. Accommodation. CH3 6AE
OLD TROOPER - canalside Bridge 122. Tel: 01244 335784. Harvester. CH3 6AE
RING O' BELLS - village centre. Tel: 01244 335422. Smartly refurbished gastro-pub which regularly wins awards. Village store opposite. CH3 7AS

29

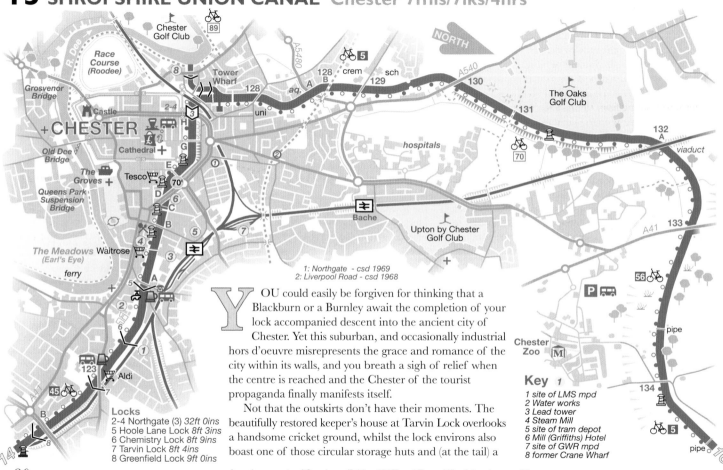

Chester Golf Club

89

NORTH

Race Course (Roodee)

5

128

crem

sch

A540

130

The Oaks Golf Club

Tower Wharf

128

aq. A

128 B

129

131

132 A

viaduct

Grosvenor Bridge

uni

Castle

CHESTER

2-4

H

Cathedral

G

hospitals

70

Old Dee Bridge

E

The Groves

Tesco

70'

D

C

Bache

133

Queens Park Suspension Bridge

B

Upton by Chester Golf Club

A41

The Meadows (Earl's Eye)

Waitrose

5

7

ferry

4

3

1: Northgate - csd 1969
2: Liverpool Road - csd 1968

Chester Zoo

M

56

A

2

6

123

Aldi

45

7

B

14

8

30

Locks
2-4 Northgate (3) 32ft 0ins
5 Hoole Lane Lock 8ft 3ins
6 Chemistry Lock 8ft 9ins
7 Tarvin Lock 8ft 4ins
8 Greenfield Lock 9ft 0ins

pipe

134

P

pipe

5

16

Key 1
1 site of LMS mpd
2 Water works
3 Lead tower
4 Steam Mill
5 site of tram depot
6 Mill (Griffiths) Hotel
7 site of GWR mpd
8 former Crane Wharf

Y OU could easily be forgiven for thinking that a Blackburn or a Burnley await the completion of your lock accompanied descent into the ancient city of Chester. Yet this suburban, and occasionally industrial hors d'oeuvre misrepresents the grace and romance of the city within its walls, and you breath a sigh of relief when the centre is reached and the Chester of the tourist propaganda finally manifests itself.

Not that the outskirts don't have their moments. The beautifully restored keeper's house at Tarvin Lock overlooks a handsome cricket ground, whilst the lock environs also boast one of those circular storage huts and (at the tail) a

for enlargements of Cow Lane (Bridge 123E) and Tower Wharf, turn to page 35

former mill now occupied by a dealer in used cars. Chemistry Lock (which is said to have gained its unusual name from the proximity of a works producing gallic acid for use in the tanning industry) is overlooked by Boughton Waterworks, itself dominated by an impressively cylindrical water tower dating from the 1850s. The city's domestic water supplies are pumped up from the River Dee, only a few hundred yards away at this point. The terraced houses on the opposite bank of the canal front onto a street prosaically named Watertower View; shades of Railway Cuttings, East Cheam. Indeed, its neighbour is Railway Terrace, a reminder that Chester's LMS motive power depot, 6A, stood nearby. In the immortal words of R. S. Grimsley - who heroically compiled a complete guide to the location of all the main locomotive sheds and works in Great Britain - the depot lay 'at the end of a cinder path' off Hoole Lane. Didn't they all!

Such scenes contextualise this once heavily industrialised quarter of Chester. Further evidence coming in the lofty shape of a lead shot tower (originally used for making musket shot during the Napoleonic Wars) and numerous warehouses, timber yards, chemical works and mills (now converted into flats and pubs and clubs) which shoulder-barge the canal as it passes through an area of the city once vital to the coffers of the Shropshire Union. All that's missing are the cargo vessels which thronged the canal. Their crews would rub their eyes in surprise at holidaymaking boaters emerging from Waitrose laden with delicacies for dinner, or diners aboard the Mill Hotel's restaurant boat, which at least maintains a wide-beam tradition more in keeping with the Chester Canal's working past

Hoole Lane Lock

Frost's Mill

than the ubiquitous narrow boats of the present day.

Beyond Tarvin Road Bridge, No.123, the numbering sequence turns to alphabetical suffixes, a sure sign that the bridges were erected after the canal was originally completed, illustrating the rapid growth of Chester in the 19th century. Either side of Cow Lane Bridge (123E - a popular mooring zone whose name recalls the site of a cattle market), side arms extended into covered basins in the heyday of the canal; the approach to a side-bridge spanning the westernmost of these may still be discerned where the council have attractively landscaped the area between the canal and the wall to create a pleasant sward known as King Charles Tower Garden.

It is the canal's juxtaposition with Chester's cathedral and its largely medieval but occasionally Roman wall, however, which is arguably its most memorable gesture. The round tower from which King Charles I watched his Cavaliers retreating raggedly from Rowton Moor looms out over the water so dramatically that the canal resembles a moat, which is exactly what it once was, and the canal builders took good advantage of this defensive channel. Canyon-like, the canal parallels the city wall and proceeds beneath Northgate spanned by a slender footbridge across which condemned prisoners were lead from the city's gaol to the Bluecoat Chapel to receive their last rites.

Some boaters may be feeling almost as nervous at the prospect of Northgate Locks as prisoners facing eternity. A gargantuan staircase, hewn out of solid sandstone and noisily bookended by the inner ring road (opened - doubtless with a pretty shake of her strawberry blonde bouffant

Bridge 123J

Tower Wharf

Cow Lane

hairdo - by Barbara Castle on 22nd April 1966) and the railway, they are ponderous in operation, but quietly satisfying to complete. The flight's three massive, and intrinsically gaol-like chambers lower the canal over thirty feet. Originally there were five of them, leading direct to the Dee. Lock-keepers are often on hand to help these days, but don't necessarily bank on one being there.

Tower Wharf rewards those who have persevered through Northgate Locks with a canalscape overlooked by new apartment blocks yet still brimming with interest: Telford's warehouse (now an eponymous and justifiably popular pub) with its arched loading bay; the adjoining Raymond (previously Harvest) House, erstwhile offices of the Chester Canal Co. and departure point of packet boats to Ellesmere Port; an elegantly canopied drydock; a large boatyard, where the Shropshire Union carrying fleet was once built and maintained; and the rare fascination of two adjacent canal levels side by side. The former North Basin -

thoughtlessly infilled in the Fifties - has been re-dug and re-watered as part of a redevelopment scheme. A plaque on Bridge 126 appropriately commemorates Lionel Thomas Caswell Rolt's championing of the canals, for he was born in Chester in 1910.

Canal boaters have long harboured covetous thoughts concerning the River Dee. True, it has always been theoretically feasible to negotiate the Dee Branch from Tower Wharf and, with the help of a high spring tide, negotiate Chester Weir to reach the calmer waters of the Upper Dee, explorable for a dozen picturesque miles upstream to Farndon. But that has always been a hazardous passage, reliant on experienced boating skills and the stamina to deal with the bureaucracy of two navigational authorities. Little wonder, then, that in recent years the final lock into the river has become semi-derelict.

Amongst other interested parties, Chester Canal Heritage Trust are advocating a revitalised link between the canal and the non-tidal Dee, key to which is the provision of a new lock in a former mill race adjoining the weir. An ambitious, yet praiseworthy scheme, eminently achievable were

Telford's Warehouse

engineering the only challenge. Eminently desirable too, for, the Dee is undeniably picturesque: witness the resort-like Groves, which does a passable imitation of Henley on a hot summer afternoon.

Meanwhile, in the event of a tedious hiatus between promotion and realisation, we would advocate perambulation of the excellent Riverside Promenade Trail which will give you a willow-framed flavour of the river between the Dee Branch and The Groves. En route you will be introduced to Crane Wharf, which flourished in the 18th century before the river began silting up, and which in latter years was the base of Crosville, the much mourned independent operator of bus services throughout North Wales and Cheshire; to Chester Race Course, one of Britain's oldest and shortest, an anti-clockwise flat course graced by an elegant grandstand; a railway bridge designed by Robert Stephenson which once fell down; to the Grosvenor Bridge of 1832 which briefly boasted the widest arch in the world; to the Old Dee Bridge which dates from the 14th century; and

to the aforementioned Groves, a pleasure resort par excellence which, when it isn't acting like it's on the Thames, imagines it's on the Seine. Who wouldn't relish boating past such treasures!

Downstream, it is another matter, the tidal Dee surges to and fro along a channel dug in the 18th century in an ultimately futile attempt to prolong Chester's role as a port. In the Middle Ages it had rivalled Bristol, but had fallen into decline, hence opening of the Wirral Line of the Ellesmere Canal in 1795. Oddly, there is a semblance of commercial activity downstream where Airbus wings are conveyed by barge from Broughton to Mostyn for transhipment onto a sea-going vessel for transport to France.

Photogenically framed by a drydock and a graceful, curving footbridge (No.126) what is generally known as Taylor's Boatyard was originally the Shropshire Union's extensive boatbuilding and maintenance yard. Facilities included three covered slipways (of which one remains), a sawmill, smithy,

The Dee Branch

and paintshop. In excess of seventy men were employed in the construction and repair of both wide beam flats and narrowboats, among the latter being *Saturn*, the restored flyboat, built here in 1906. Under London & North Western Railway ownership, the Shropshire Union's fleet of over five hundred vessels appeared secure. Yet in 1921, a sudden decision was made to cease carrying and disband the fleet. Determination, by the Government, for a 56 hour working week (effectively a maximum of 8 hours a day) rendered boat operation unviable overnight. The yard was acquired by a local boatbuilding family called Taylor, who operated the business for the next fifty years. Taylors turned their hand to a wide range of vessels, commercial, leisure and even military. Of particular appeal was a series of classic wooden cabin cruisers, one of which, *Amaryllis*, is on display at the National Waterways Museum, Ellesmere Port. Taylors sold out to Bithells in the 1970s and subsequently the yard was taken over by David Jones. These days it belongs to the Askey family, the yard's historic buildings have acquired listed status, and a firm sense of tradition continues.

The Wirral Line of the Ellesmere Canal, a constituent of the Shrop-shire Union, wriggles out of the city's suburbs. Girls come giggling out of Chester University's Parkgate Road Campus as if auditioning for extras in Channel 4's Chester based soap *Hollyoaks*. Bridge 128A carries the canal over the A5480 link road: in more ways than one, it is an elevating experience to glide on water over queuing road traffic. Bridge 128B bears National Cycle Route 5, formerly the Great Central Railway's line from Chester Northgate to Wrexham. Chester's crematorium lies alongside Bridge 129. The towpath is popular with cyclists, and soon the landscape opens out, though not necessarily agriculturally, much of the offside being bounded by a golf course.

A fine sandstone viaduct (132A) conveys the railway between Chester and Birkenhead, the preserve of scurrying third-rail electric units now, but once the route of Great Western expresses and sleeper trains carrying passengers to catch Transatlantic liners from the Mersey. Up on the neighbouring hillside stands a neo-classical house called Friars Park; perhaps designed by Lutyens, but more likely inspired by him. Visitor moorings by Bridge 134 offer the opportunity to visit Chester Zoo.

Chester   Map 15

On Sunday mornings, Chester breathes like a sleeping child and footsteps echo your progress around the city wall, the perfect introduction to this lovely city. At most other times, though, shoppers and tourists transform Chester into a frenetic, free-for-all from which you are apt to go scurrying back to your boat for refuge. But in all of Britain's inland waterways, only York can vie with Chester when it comes to antiquity, and the city wall, which kept enemies at bay down the centuries, now keeps 21st century reality in its place. Once through the ancient gateways you are wrapped in a medieval time warp which makes Chester the most agreeable of places to saunter in and absorb the atmosphere.

It was the Romans who founded the city, seeing it as a likely place to build a port and keep a weather eye on the troublesome Marches; they called it Deva. In the Dark Ages the Anglo Saxons undid much of their predecessors' civilisation, but by the Middle Ages Chester was flourishing again and a 12th century writer noted ships from Aquitaine, Germany and Spain berthed in the shadow of the city wall. Chester's celebrated 'Rows' are thought to have had their origins during this period. These covered galleries above street level are quite unique, and elevate window-shopping into a pleasurable experience for all and sundry.

During the Civil War the city supported King Charles, but it did him little good for it was from the walls of Chester that he saw his army defeated on Rowton Heath. Victorian Chester grew up outside the city wall, beyond the canal and out towards the railway. What the Victorians did inside the wall is best forgotten by those romantics who like to think that all that black and white half timbering is original.

Eating & Drinking

JOSEPH BENJAMIN - Northgate Street. Tel: 01244 344295. Excellent Michelin and *Good Food Guide* listed restaurant open daily (ex Mon) for breakfast and lunch and for dinner Thur-Sat. CH1 2HT
BLACKSTOCKS - Northgate Street. Tel: 01244 325822. Eat in or take-away fish & chips open daily from 11.30am. CH1 2HQ
THE BREWERY TAP - Lower Bridge Street. Tel: 01244 340999. Good food (noon to 9.30pm daily) and locally brewed ales (plus guests) from Waverton in ancient high-ceilinged house. *Good Beer Guide* entry. CH1 1RU
CHEZ JOULES - Northgate Street. Tel: 01244 400014. French restaurant with emphasis on seasonal produce. Tempting Thursday soiree cinema. CH1 2HQ

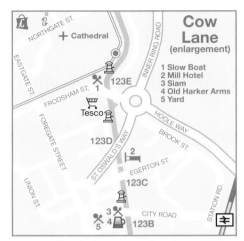

Cow Lane
(enlargement)

1 Slow Boat
2 Mill Hotel
3 Siam
4 Old Harker Arms
5 Yard

man make of it? Weetwood beers from Tarporley. *Good Beer Guide* entry. CH1 4EZ
THE YARD - City Road (Bridge 123B). Tel: 01244 325199. Modern Italian Dining. CH1 2AE

Shopping

One of the most amenable shopping centres in Britain. The Rows contain some of the most up-market shops in the city within their fascinating galleries, whilst St Michael's Arcade is a Victorian confection of soaring iron and glass reached off Bridge Street Row. At the opposite end of the retail spectrum is Chester's fine indoor market, open Mon-Sat, 8am-5pm, where stalls specialise in fresh Cheshire produce. Don't miss the marvellous Cheese Shop (Tel: 01244 314659 - CH1 2HT) on Northgate. There's a Waitrose supermarket canalside between bridges 123A & B, and a Tesco on Frodsham Street adjoining Bridge 123E. Finally, if you're moored at Tower Wharf, useful facilities on nearby Garden Lane (access via Bridge 126E) include two convenience stores, a butcher, fast food outlets and a launderette.

Things to Do

VISITOR INFORMATION CENTRE - Town Hall, Northgate. Tel: 0845 647 7868. CH1 2HS
CHESTER CATHEDRAL - One of England's ecclesiastical masterpieces. Tel: 01244 324756. Gift shop and cafe. CH1 2HU
DEWA ROMAN EXPERIENCE - Pierpoint Lane. Tel: 01244 343407. Open daily 9am-5pm. Roman remains! CH1 1NL
GROSVENOR MUSEUM - Grosvenor Street. Museum of local history. Admission free, open daily. Tel: 01244 972197. CH1 2DD
CITY SIGHTSEEING - open-top bus tours. Tel: 01244 381461.
CHESTER HERITAGE TOURS - city tours aboard replica 1910 'B-Type' open-top bus. Tel: 0844 585 4144.

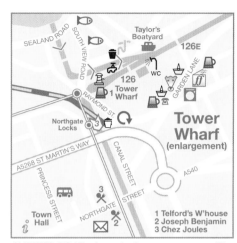

Tower Wharf
(enlargement)

1 Telford's W'house
2 Joseph Benjamin
3 Chez Joules

MAD HATTERS - Bridge Street Row East. Tel: 01244 323444. Avowedly eccentric tearoom housed in former rectory, open from breakfast onwards. Beautifully designed cakes. CH1 1NW
MILL HOTEL - by Bridge 123C. Tel: 01244 350035. Restaurant, bar food and a bewildering choice of real ale. Restaurant boat. *GBG* listed. CH1 3NF
OLD HARKER ARMS - City Road (Bridge 123B). Tel: 01244 344525. Well-appointed warehouse conversion. *Good Beer Guide* entry. Wide range of real ales and good choice of food. CH3 5AL. *Up the steps on City Road stand a plethora of ethnic restaurants.*
SIAM - City Road. (Bridge 123B). Tel: 01244 403222. Thai and Teppan-yaki restaurant. CH1 3AE
SLOW BOAT - Frodsham Street (Bridge 123E). Tel: 01244 317873. Canalside Asian fusion. CH1 3JJ
TELFORD'S WAREHOUSE - Tower Wharf (Bridge 123L). Tel: 01244 390090. Eat and drink in Telford's handsome canal warehouse - what would the great

CHESTER BOAT - from the boating station on The Groves aboard Bithells launches. Tel: 01244 325394. CH1 1SD
CHESTER ZOO - One of Europe's finest zoos. Admission charge, open daily. Best reached from the canal via Bridge 134. Tel: 01244 380280. CH2 1EU
MILITARY MUSEUM - Chester Castle. Tel: 01244 327617. CH1 2DN

Connections

BUSES - bus station on George Street off Northgate. Tel: 0871 200 2233. Service 1 runs every 20 minutes (hourly Sun) to Ellesmere Port, a 35 minute ride away. Service 84 (hourly, daily) shadows the Shropshire Union most of the way down to Nantwich.
TRAINS - railway station on City Road, reached from Bridge 123B. Tel: 03457 484950. Free bus link to city centre for rail ticket holders.
TAXIS - Chester Radio Taxis. Tel: 01244 372372.

EVER so slightly smug, you are entitled to feel, having left Chester and its holidaymakers behind, to steer along a broad-beam canal in the historic wake of steam powered flats hastening back across the Mersey to Liverpool for another cargo of imported grain. Or you may prefer to be driving the horse of a flyboat across the Wirral's wrist to Ellesmere Port with Walsall manufactured spurs for export to Argentina. Your fantasies can be further indulged at the admirable (if sadly under-funded) National Waterways Museum, or Boat Museum as diehards continue to call it ... well, some of your fantasies, anyway.

But first comes a salutary reminder, in the shape of a complex motorway intersection, that this is the age of the car and the juggernaut lorry and that water as a mode of transport has, by and large, been irrationally consigned to the past. All but throttled by sliproads, the village of Stoak seems understandably traumatised by the cacophony on its doorstep, the crenellated tower of St Lawrence's church offering up a prayer for survival. Incidentally, a hire boat called *The Rambler*, based at Stoak in the 1930s, may even have predated those available at Christleton on Map 14.

With the jagged, Iron Age fort topped outline of Helsby Hill prominent to the north-east, the gleaming refineries of Stanlow define themselves on the horizon. Stanlow, opened in the 1920s, is second only to Fawley on The Solent in output, and provides a sixth of Britain's petroleum requirements. In the 12th century there was an

Boaters may shun this length of waterway, but the towpath is metalled throughout and popular with walkers and cyclists alike: disparate lifeforms who appear to co-exist fairly harmoniously; up this way at any rate.

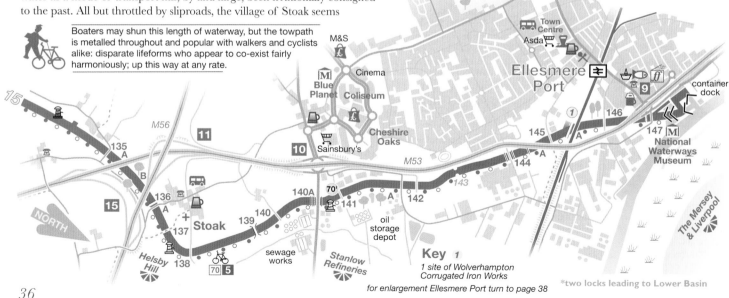

Key 1
1 site of Wolverhampton
Corrugated Iron Works

for enlargement Ellesmere Port turn to page 38

*two locks leading to Lower Basin

abbey on the banks of the Mersey. But life there was too bleak for even its hair-shirted inhabitants, and they moved to new premises near Clitheroe in Lancashire in 1287.

Car showrooms either side of Bridge 140A run the gamut from Skoda to BMW, with Harley-Davidson motorbikes thrown in for good measure. Visitor moorings offer the opportunity for you to step out of the 19th century straight into the 21st in the form of Cheshire Oaks, Europe's first designer outlet village and still the largest in the UK. After Bridge 145 a huge wasteground is all that remains of the once gargantuan Wolverhampton Corrugated Iron Works. The company moved here in 1905, and it is said that some of its two thousand strong workforce simply walked up the Shropshire Union Canal's towpath to their new abode.

For boaters intending to stay just a short time in the vicinity, limited mooring space is usually available between the motorway bridge and the National Waterways Museum. Preferable though, in our opinion, are the

Ellesmere Port - After

Ellesmere Port - Before

spacious moorings in the lower basin reached through the locks. To access them you will have to report to the museum's reception desk and pay, but in with the price comes the novel feeling that, temporarily at least, you and your boat have become one of the prize exhibits.

Ellesmere Port, the 'port' of the Ellesmere Canal, dates from the last decade of the 18th century. The Wirral Line of the Ellesmere Canal met the Mersey here at what had, until then, been simply the small village of Netherpool. The opening of the Birmingham & Liverpool Junction Canal and later the Manchester Ship Canal turned these docks into a transhipment complex of almost unique significance. Abandoned in 1958 and suffering neglect typical of the 1960s, Ellesmere Port's darkest hour came in 1970 when Telford's superb 'Winged Warehouses' - three blocks of four storey structures which spanned the lower basin - were destroyed by fire. The Holiday Inn which occupies the location now provides a pale replacement. Fortunately, five enthusiasts - Harry Arnold, Peter Froud, Tony Lewery, David Owen and Edward Paget-Tomlinson - were sufficiently prescient to form what was originally known as the North West Museum of Inland Navigation. Heroes to a man!

Stoak
Map 16

Soporific rural community despite presence of motorways on its doorstep.

Eating & Drinking
BUNBURY ARMS - village centre, access via bridges 136 or 137. Tel: 01244 301665. Country pub offering lunches, evening meals and Sunday roasts. CH2 4HW

Connections
BUSES - service No. 26 runs Mon-Fri to/from Chester & Ellesmere Port. Tel: 0871 200 2233.

Ellesmere Port
Map 16

A 'cup tie' town of two halves, with a bit of extra time bolted on. Terraced streets fan out from the canal, still backing onto cobbled alleyways. Strung out along Station Road are tattoo parlours, tanning studios, pawnbrokers and accident claim solicitors. Selwyn Lloyd, Chancellor of the Exchequer (and a Wirral lad, to boot) unveiled Westminster Bridge in 1961. It carries you across the railway into a second half of unconsidered concrete and a 'time-wasting' shopping mall. Extra time takes place out by Junction 10, where The Coliseum retail park boasts the biggest Marks & Spencer outside of London. Follow the money!

Eating & Drinking
ESSENCE OF SPICE - Whitby Road. Tel: 0151 355 9596. If in doubt, eat Indian! Open from 5pm Mon-Sat and 1pm Sun. CH65 8AB

THE GALLEY - South Pier Road. Tel: 0151 355 1163. Cafe/restaurant adjacent museum. CH65 4FW

THE THOMAS TELFORD - Whitby Road (town centre). Tel: 0151 350 3740. Wetherspoons. CH65 8AB

WATERSIDE CAFE - National Waterways Museum. Tel: 0151 355 5017. Open 10am-4pm daily throughout the year. CH65 4FW

Cheshire Oaks hosts a wide range of chain restaurants: Cafe Rouge, Harvester, Nandos, Prezzo, Wagamama etc.

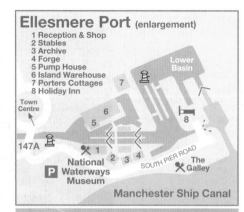

Ellesmere Port (enlargement)

1 Reception & Shop
2 Stables
3 Archive
4 Forge
5 Pump House
6 Island Warehouse
7 Porters Cottages
8 Holiday Inn

Lower Basin

Town Centre

147A

National Waterways Museum

SOUTH PIER ROAD

The Galley

Manchester Ship Canal

Fore & Aft

Shopping
Five minutes walk (through a seedy underpass) takes you to a convenience store. Ten minutes and you'll reach the Market Hall (closed Weds), an Aldi and a large Asda. From the visitor moorings between bridges 140A and 141 Sainsbury's is easily reached.

Things to Do
THE NATIONAL WATERWAYS MUSEUM - South Pier Road. Tel: 0151 355 5017. Open daily 10am-5pm mid February to December. Admission charge. Along with Gloucester and Stoke Bruerne in Northamptonshire, this is one of three Canal & River Trust operated museum sites. Each has its own unique atmosphere. Here, a dockland setting hosts a collection of narrow and widebeam inland waterway craft, though the sad truth that not all of them are in a good state of health only serves to illustrate the time-consuming and expensive challenge of keeping such invaluable examples of waterway heritage afloat. Exhibition Hall, Engine House, Historic Cottages, Stables and Forge. Cafe and shop. Boat trips along the Shropshire Union. Secure moorings, water and refuse facilities provided for visiting boaters. CH65 4FW

BLUE PLANET AQUARIUM - Cheshire Oaks. Tel: 0151 357 8804. Deepwater antidote to the inherent shallowness of all canals. CH65 9LF

Connections
BUSES - First service 1 links Ellesmere Port with Liverpool and Chester every 20 minutes Mon-Sat (hourly Sun) calling usefully en route at Cheshire Oaks Designer Outlet, the Blue Planet Aquarium, and Chester Zoo. Tel: 0871 200 2233.

TRAINS - frequent services to Liverpool via Birkenhead and Chester (change at Hooton). Tel: 03457 484950.

TAXIS - Cozey Cars. Tel: 0151 355 4040.

Llangollen Canal

Grindley Brook

BRITAIN'S most popular canal - picture *Strictly Come Dancing* with boats - hits the ground running at Hurleston Junction. Four closely spaced locks kick-start a forty-five mile journey from Cheshire's farmland to the mountains of Wales, and things can get tense. Boats may pass in the short and deceptively shallow intervening pounds between the somewhat restricted ('Please Lift Your Fenders' in place of 'Please Mind My Sequins') chambers, but a certain degree of unwritten protocol and etiquette should be displayed if tempers aren't to fray. 'After you, Claude' is the best approach, and be nice to all the other boaters you encounter; well, Canal Companion users anyway.

Adjoining the locks, a reservoir stores water which has flowed down the canal from the River Dee at Horseshoe Falls above Llangollen, before being treated and piped to the kitchen sinks of Crewe. Thank your lucky stars for this water; without it, the London Midland & Scottish Railway would have closed the canal during the Second World War, when they thought no one would be looking. In fact, technically the canal was 'abandoned' and it was only its use as a water channel that saved it from the dereliction suffered by other LMS owned waterways under an infamous Act of 1944.

Gradually, a new traffic of pleasure boats began using the canal, and under the 1968 Transport Act the Llangollen Canal (as the section of the old Ellesmere Canal between Hurleston and Llangollen had become known) was classified a 'cruiseway', its position as one of the premier canal holiday routes assured for posterity.

Wherein lies the Llangollen's appeal? Well it doesn't do it any harm that it never gets suburban, let alone urban or industrialised, and there can't be many canal routes that can lay claim to that. Furthermore the fact that it sets off from England in search of Wales gives it a sense of purpose ironically at odds with its ad hoc origins. Crusty old canal salts will tell you it's overrated, but we'll let *you* be the judge of that! What is noticeable, is a preponderance of hire boats over privately owned craft.

Intuitively, one expects to be travelling East to West, but, initially the canal runs, disconcertingly, on a North-South axis. A rural atmosphere is rapidly established. Big farms like Bache House hint at an intensity of agriculture past its zenith. From bridges 3 and 4 footpaths lead enticingly across the pastures to Park Farm where the Sadler family's three daughters make and sell delicious Snugburys ice cream.

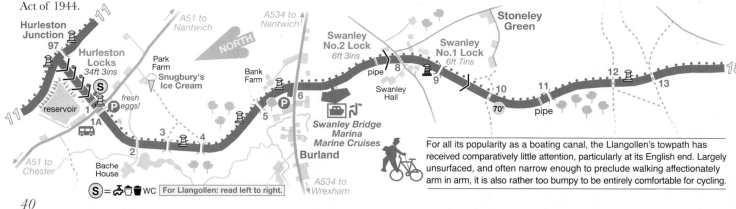

For all its popularity as a boating canal, the Llangollen's towpath has received comparatively little attention, particularly at its English end. Largely unsurfaced, and often narrow enough to preclude walking affectionately arm in arm, it is also rather too bumpy to be entirely comfortable for cycling.

(S) = 🚰🏕🗑💧 WC | For Llangollen: read left to right.

At Burland, an old estate village on the Nantwich to Wrexham main road, a rectangle of water denotes a former wharf. But the canal's prosperity these days comes from the berthing of boats, as at Swanley Marina, rather than the delivery and despatch of goods. Interestingly, though we tend to think of narrowboats carrying single cargoes of mostly bulky commodities such as coal, chemicals or minerals, up until the sudden demise of the Shropshire Union fleet in 1921 hundreds of horse-drawn boats plied the system bearing a huge variety of daily necessities; the ubiquitous DHL and UPS logistics vans of their day: all delivered - albeit scarcely credible - without the aid of GPS. Swanley Hall is another substantial farm. Like Hurleston, the locks at Swanley and Baddiley (Map 18) can become congested at busy times. Bridge 11 features brickwork embossed with the manufacturer's name: 'Wood & Ivery, Albion Brick Works, West Bromwich'.

The flow of water down the Llangollen Canal increases the running of the by-washes, causing a gush of water to run across the canal at the foot of locks. To compensate, steer slightly into the overflow. Going downhill, avoid being drawn over to the cill of the by-weir. Also bear in mind that - like a river with a current - your boat will travel slightly faster on its way back down the canal. The times quoted at the top of each map are averaged out. Add a bit when going towards Wales, subtract a bit on the way back.

Hurleston Locks

Hurleston Junction

WRENBURY is one of the most picturesque ports of call at the English end of the Llangollen Canal. Bridge 20, rebuilt in timber and electrified (operated with a CRT Yale key), is equipped with less than discreet traffic lights but it would take more than these to spoil the attractive scene presented by the canal wharf and its old

base and a canal shop, and self-catering accommodation.

Wrenbury Hall's history goes back to Domesday but the present mock Elizabethan mansion dates from 1919. In living memory it has been used to rehabilitate tuberculosis sufferers and as a training centre for ambulance personnel, but now it promotes itself as 'South Cheshire's most desirable wedding venue'. The residing family's motto was *Riget Otio Virtus*. Fluency in Latin being taken for granted where Canal Companion users are concerned, it is hardly necessary to translate this as 'virtue becomes stiff with idleness' - rather like some paddle gear we could mention.

Either side of Wrenbury, the Llangollen Canal wends its way through peaceful countryside of considerable charm. About a mile and a half or so to the south-east stands an obelisk in the landscaped grounds of Combermere Abbey, a substantial house developed on the site of a Cistercian monastery abandoned at the time of The Dissolution. The monument commemorates one Stapleton Cotton, a distinguished soldier who served under the Duke of Wellington who visited the house in 1820. Amongst other recreational activities, Combermere is now used as a venue for - how did you guess? - weddings!

mills, now used as a pub and boatyard. The older of the two buildings dates back to the opening of the canal, though its site was used for a mill as early as the 16th century, power coming from the adjoining waters of the stripling Weaver. On the opposite bank, the more modern mill belongs to the 20th century, being constructed in a surprisingly effective combination of corrugated iron and mellow brick. The former miller, Arthur Sumner, once operated a small fleet of narrowboats, acquired out of necessity when the Shropshire Union ceased carrying in 1921. Sumner's boats were immaculately turned out with red cabin sides, Tuscan lettering and a profusion of roses and castles. When lorries inevitably took over from the boats, their livery was equally attractive, if somewhat less ornate. Descendants of Arthur Sumner were landlords at the Dusty Miller until 2011. Nowadays, appropriately enough, the younger mill serves as a hire fleet

1 Blind bend
2 CRT facilities Yale key required for Bridge 20

Wrenbury
Map 18

A straggling but pleasant village in the civil parish of Wrenbury cum Frith. What centre there is adjoins a green. The church (whose mellifluous chimes can be heard from the canal) and school are its most notable buildings. A strong community spirit manifests itself in the annual, and hugely imaginative scarecrow trail.

Eating & Drinking
COTTON ARMS - adjacent Bridge 20. Tel: 01270 780377. A favourite with boaters campers and caravanners. Food and real ale. CW5 8HG
DUSTY MILLER - canalside Bridge 20. Tel: 01270 780537. Comfortably furnished pub (closed Mon) occupying a converted mill. Wide choice of food (including breakfast from 9.30am Sat & Sun) and Robinsons ales from Stockport. CW5 8HG

Shopping
Farm shop (ex Mon) canalside at the Dusty Miller.

Well-stocked post office stores down by the village green, five minutes walk from the canal. Open from 7.30am to 8pm Mon-Sat and 8.30am to 8pm Sun. Hot take-away food counter. Tel: 01270 780228.

Things to Do
SNUGBURY'S - Park Farm (access from bridges 3 or 4, Map 17). Tel: 01270 624830. Farm based ice cream parlour. 9.30am to 6pm (5pm winter). CW5 6BU

Self-Catering
ABC offer self-catering for up to four people in an apartment in Wrenbury Mill - Tel: 0330 333 0590.

Connections
TRAINS - roughly bi-hourly Arriva Trains Wales services to/from Crewe and Shrewsbury via Whitchurch and Nantwich. Tel: 03457 484950.
BUSES - service 72 operates four times daily (ex Sun) to/from Nantwich and Whitchurch (via Marbury). Tel: 0871 200 2233.

Marbury
Map 19

One of those 'quietest places under the sun' that we all dream of retiring to. The church lych-gate celebrates "Ye who live mid English pastures green". Below the village are two meres. A footpath leads down to the larger and you can watch the antics of the wildfowl from its reedy banks. There's a secluded seat in the churchyard overlooking Big Mere.

Eating & Drinking
THE SWAN INN - village centre. Tel: 01948 666870. Pleasant country pub 5 minutes walk from Bridges 23 or 24. Closed all day Mon, and Tue lunchtimes. Food lunch & dinner Wed-Sat and Sun lunch. SY13 4LS

Things to Do
BARN BOOKS - Pear Tree Farm. Tel: 01948 663742. Dealer in antiquarian, second-hand and new books. Open Fri-Sun 10am-5pm and also by prior appointment. SY13 4HZ

Wrenbury Mill

GRINDLEY BROOK is the focal point of this part of the Llangollen Canal. Here are six locks in close proximity, three of them forming a substantial 'staircase' overlooked by a splendid round-bayed lock-keeper's house typical of Telford's architectural style. In fact, the interest at Grindley Brook starts below the bottom lock where a fine skew bridge of blue engineering bricks baked in Rowley Regis still carries the track-bed of the old Chester to Whitchurch railway over the canal. A trio of single chambers precedes the stair-case, the bottom of which is spanned by the Chester road, and bordered by old mill buildings.

The activity at Grindley Brook on a Bank Holiday weekend or busy summer's day provides wonderful entertainment for the spectator, if not the imperturbable lock-keeper who is on duty daily from 8.30am April to October. The stair-case locks, in particular, cause considerable congestion: Sundays and Mondays are busiest for ascending boats; Thursdays and Fridays for descending boats. Delays in excess of two hours are not unheard of, though it is worth bearing in mind that mornings are less busy than after-noons, from which one can only conclude that modern day boaters are a load of lazy lie-ins. People react to the hold ups in different ways: some with frustration, some with saintly resignation.

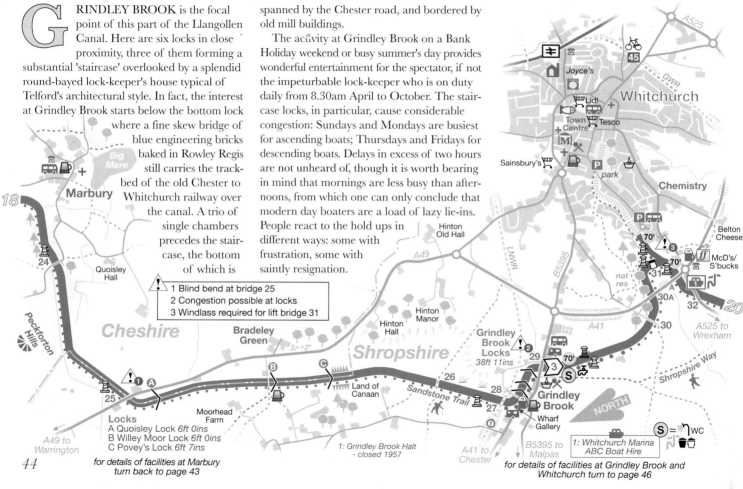

1 Blind bend at bridge 25
2 Congestion possible at locks
3 Windlass required for lift bridge 31

Locks
A Quoisley Lock *6ft 0ins*
B Willey Moor Lock *6ft 0ins*
C Povey's Lock *6ft 7ins*

Grindley Brook Locks *38ft 11ins*

1: Grindley Brook Halt - closed 1957

1: Whitchurch Marina ABC Boat Hire

44

for details of facilities at Marbury turn back to page 43

for details of facilities at Grindley Brook and Whitchurch turn to page 46

The secret, of course, is to remember that you are on holiday and supposed to be enjoying yourself! The westbound boater, having climbed some forty feet through the six locks, does at least have twenty lock free miles to look forward to.

North of Grindley Brook the canal forms the county boundary between Cheshire and Shropshire for a short distance. The 'Sandstone Trail' swells the ranks of towpath walkers on this section. Reeds form a soothing curtain between the path and the water. The picturesque village of Marbury is shunned and the general atmosphere is one of isolation. South of Grindley Brook the canal makes as if to call at the old Shropshire market town of Whitchurch, but then seems to think better of it. A short branch terminated in the centre of town but was abandoned in 1944 and was subsequently, to the town's regret, filled in. In 1993, however, a start was made in reclaiming

Whitchurch Arm

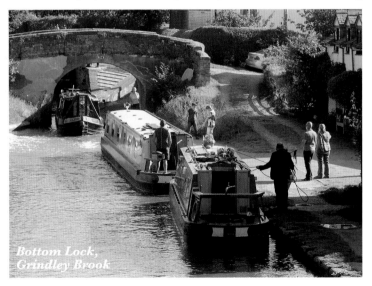

Bottom Lock,
Grindley Brook

the arm by restoring the first few hundred yards of it to provide moorings for visitors to the town. After toying with an ambitious scheme to construct an inclined plane to take the arm much nearer to the town centre, Whitchurch Canal Trust are now proposing a more modest terminal basin within the town's country park. Pending this, you can follow the well-surfaced 'Sandstone Trail' into the town, and discover the former wharf, still obvious at the far end of Jubilee Park. Up until the 1920s cheese fly-boats journeyed from Whitchurch wharf (and a number of other cheese-making towns in the district, such as Market Drayton and Nantwich) to Manchester or Ellesmere Port (for Liverpool), the cheeses being stored on shelves in a hold covered with white canvas to deflect the sun's rays. The melodramatic denouement to J. Jefferson Farjeon's 1932 novel *The Z Murders* takes place on the outskirts of Whitchurch.

Grindley Brook

Map 19

Canalside community on the A41, the old road from London to Birkenhead.

Eating & Drinking

HORSE & JOCKEY - adjacent Bridge 28. Tel: 01948 662723. *Good Beer Guide* listed renovated pub offering a good choice of food from noon daily. SY13 4QJ

LOCKSIDE CAFE - canalside by staircase locks. Tel: 01948 663385. Internet cafe offering breakfasts, filled baguettes, jacket potatoes etc. See also Lockside Stores below. SY13 4QH

WILLEY MOOR LOCK TAVERN - beside the lock. Tel: 01948 663274. Picturesque - and justifiably popular - GBG listed free house reached by motorists via a track off the A49. Good home cooked food and an interesting and ever changing range of ales. Pleasant garden with children's play area. SY13 4HF

Shopping

LOCKSIDE STORES - beside the staircase. Tel: 01948 663385. A good range of groceries. Local cheeses and meats are complimented by chutneys and jams, as well as crafts, gifts and off licence. SY13 4QH

WHARF GALLERY - canalside between bridges 27 & 28. Tel: 01948 666693. Charming outlet for Buffy Robinson who specialises in batik. SY13 4QJ

Grindley Brook also boasts a petrol station with shop backing onto the bottom lock by Bridge 28. A canalside house deals in books and crafts.

Connections

BUSES - service 41 runs approximately bi-hourly throughout the week to Whitchurch in one direction and to Chester in the other. Tel: 0871 200 2233.

Whitchurch

Map 19

'The most handsome town in north Shropshire' enthused Messrs Betjeman and Piper in their collaborative *Shell Guide* of 1951, and the sixty-five years which have elapsed since have been untypically tactful when compared to many a much spoilt market town. Architecturally, the substantial parish church of St Alkmund's leads the way, but handsome buildings are sprinkled liberally throughout. Cheese and clocks are Whitchurch's gifts to civilisation. Blue Cheshire cheese is characterised by a marbled effect and is one of the great, tangy blue cheeses in the world. Joyce's, whose clocks can be found as far away as Sydney, Shanghai and Tredegar, commenced clock making in the neighbourhood in the 17th century. Their handsome redbrick premises on Station Road were in use between 1904 and 2012, but now house the antiques showroom of Christina Trevanion & Aaron Dean, the former a frequent, not to say effervescent, guest on television antiques shows. Horologists may gain access on auction days to pay homage to Joyce's.

Eating & Drinking

COCK & GREYHOUND - Bargates (opp St Alkmund's). Tel: 01948 665151. Gastro-style refurbished pub open daily from noon. SY13 1LL

ETZIO - 60 High Street. Tel: 01948 662248. Pizza, pasta and grills just down from St Alkmund's church. Stylish interior and al fresco decking to rear. Open from 5.30pm Mon-Sat. SY13 1BB

FROLLIES - High Street. Tel: 01948 665553. Wine bar and grill open daily from 9am (10am Sun). SY13 1AZ

JONES'S - Green End. Tel: 01948 666108. Coffee shop open daily (ex Sun) 9am-4pm. SY13 1AA

HANNAH - Green End. Tel: 01948 666699. Indian restaurant (& t/a) located on first floor of former Oddfellows Hall erected 1901. SY13 1AD

OLD TOWN HALL VAULTS - St Mary's Street. Tel: 01948 664682. Cosy Joule's (of Market Drayton) pub which was the birthplace of Sir Edward German, composer of *Merrie England*, *Tom Jones*, and other light operatic works. Listed Gents loo! SY13 1QU

WALKERS - High Street. Tel: 01948 664687. Old-fashioned comfort food in beamy first-floor cafe above a bakery: infinitely maternal waitresses. SY13 1AX

There are McDonald's and Starbucks outlets on the A41 opposite Whitchurch Marina accessible via Bridge 32.

Shopping

All services in the town centre, one mile east of the canal. Friday is market day, Wednesday early closing. Farmers Market on the first Saturday in the month. Tesco supermarket by the bus station, Sainsbury's on London Road, Lidl on Bridgewater Street. Benjamin's, at the foot of High Street, is a nice deli, cafe and patisserie. Nearby, on Green End, there's a small independent bookshop punningly named Bookshrop. Wheelbase bicycle shop on Watergate Street. Bubbles launderette (ex Wed) on Station Road. There are a growing number of antiques dealers in the town. Several food shops stock locally produced Belton's cheeses. Annual Food Festival in late May.

Things to Do

HERITAGE & TOURIST INFORMATION CENTRE - St Mary's Street. Tel: 01948 664577. Exhibitions of local history and personalities such as Edward German and the Victorian illustrator Randolph Caldecott. Open Tue, Thur & Fri 11am-4pm. SY13 1QY

Connections

BUSES - service 41 links Whitchurch with Chester bi-hourly and calls at Grindley Brook en route. Service 72 runs four times daily (ex Sun) to/from Nantwich via Marbury and Wrenbury. Service 205 offers a half-hourly Mon-Sat link between the canal arm at Chemistry and the town centre bus park beside Tesco. Tel: 0871 200 2233.

TRAINS - approx bi-hourly Arriva Trains Wales services to Crewe (via Wrenbury and Nantwich) and Shrewsbury. Tel: 03457 484950.

TAXIS - ACORN TAXIS. Tel: 01948 665540.

20 LLANGOLLEN CANAL Fenn's Bank & Platt Lane 4½mls/0lks/1½hrs

BETWEEN Whitchurch (Map 19) and Ellesmere (Map 22) the Llangollen Canal encounters three distinct types of landscape: farmland, mosses, and meres. Plenty of variety, then, for those displaying withdrawal symptoms from what most would consider the blessed absence of locks. Furthermore, apart from the occasional windlass-operated lift bridge, the unencumbered boater has 'the best seat in the house' from which to enjoy the countryside's subtle scene changes.

Enjoyably undulating, the farmland appears for the most part lush and well husbanded, though burgeoning crops of maize strike an alien chord. The dynastical business of agriculture is undertaken from sizeable farmhouses bolstered by the appurtenances of different eras: handsome brick milking parlours; Dutch barns of a curious corrugated iron kind of charm; and modern day excrescences which wouldn't look out of place on an industrial estate

Through all this the canal glides serenely: occasionally in cuttings, occasionally on embankments; always with an impenetrably opaque hawthorn hedge on the towpath side. The utilitarian ranks of soil-sapping maize are relieved, here and there, by

conversation-provoking points of interest. Pan Castle marks the enigmatic remains of a motte & bailey structure which - Derrick Pratt speculates in his notes acompanying the Godfrey Edition Ordnance Survey map of Whitchurch dated 1899 - may have been erected circa 1102 by the Pandolfs of Wem. Blackoe Cottages, we *do* know, were built to provide accommodation for canal lengthsmen, and there was stabling here for boat horses as well. Metal footbridge 35 carries a branch of the Shropshire Way over the canal. The flat concrete span of Bridge 39 remains surprisingly in place, as if some benign ferroequinological deity plans to reinstate the Cambrian Railways route from Whitchurch to Oswestry. Prior to closure of the railway in 1965, Whitchurch and Ellesmere were twenty-five minutes away from each other by train. Thereafter buses, crammed with garrulous market day pensioners, took twice as long but maintained the semblance of a link.

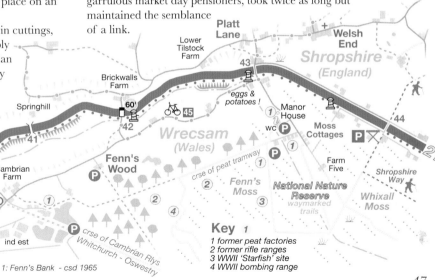

Key
1 former peat factories
2 former rifle ranges
3 WWII 'Starfish' site
4 WWII bombing range

Nowadays, motorists apart - and Pearson's have never knowingly pandered to that lamentable strata of society - transport between the two market towns, barely a dozen miles apart, has regressed to the 19th century heyday of the canal.

Not all the variations are nature's, for the canal finds itself paralleling (and briefly crossing on Map 21) the border between England and Wales, the latter being part of what used to be known as the English Maelor, or Flintshire Detached. This curious little pocket of Welshness dates back to Edward I's carving up of the Welsh principalities and Henry VIII's subsequent suppression of the Marcher Lords. Such tinkering continues, for, latterly part of Clwyd, this part of Flintshire is now administered by the County Borough of Wrexham. However life's organizers want to carve it up, though, it remains demonstrably exciting to feel oneself on the cusp of the Celtic country, as if noticing for the first time, the presence of someone you are destined to become much more intimate with. There are limekilns in the spacious garden of the house beside Bridge 42. A lifting structure of dubious reliability, it is painted a dull green; though at least it is spared the blotchy, flaking and frankly disgraceful paintwork that characterizes many of its supposedly black and white cousins.

At Platt Lane the eerie, other-worldly atmosphere of the mosses begins to impinge itself upon the canal. At over two thousand acres, they represent the third largest raised bog, or mire in lowland Britain; only Thorne Moors and Hatfield Chase near Doncaster in Yorkshire are larger. Peat began to form in the vicinity circa BC 8500 and had perhaps created its fully formed 'dome' by AD 500. Picture it as a giant blister, which remained effectively unpunctured until peat extraction for use as fuel began tentatively

Platt Lane

in the 16th century. This began an ongoing process of drainage which caused the dome to gradually subside. Prior to that the surface of the mosses would have been some thirty feet higher than now. Construction of the canal and railway in the 19th century hastened the speed of change, particularly as the transport they offered encouraged commercial peat cutting to increase. The gradual mechanisation of the process from the day when hand cut turves (measuring roughly 9 by 7 by 4 inches) were eloquently known by their size and colour as 'Whixall Bibles', to the arrival in the late 1960s of peat cutting machinery from Germany exacerbated the decline of the mosses as a natural phenomenon, for they were being pretty much destroyed for commercial gain. Moreover, not content with exploiting the mosses for fuel, horticultural products and as an unlikely source of inedible bedding for horses, use was found for them in both world wars, initially as rifle ranges and subsequently for bomb practice and as a decoy site which could be set ablaze to mislead enemy aircraft crews that they were really over Merseyside.

Now, saner policies pertain, and the mosses are conspicuously empty of human activity; almost, if one dare say it, to the point where it is missed. Under the stewardship of Natural England and Natural Resources Wales the mosses are being restored and cherished as a wetland site of international significance. Often, such scientific credentials sound ever so slightly uninspiring but, trust us, the mosses exude a character all their own, and a network of signposted trails centred on the Manor House National Nature Reserve base near Bridge 43 encourages closer exploration and appreciation. We commend to you *A Peat Cutter's Life*, a book published in 2012 in which Bill Allmark relates to Jeff Beard his vivid experiences of a working life on the mosses. It is obtainable (while stocks last) from the Manor House price £10.

THE MOSSES

BATTING its eyelids demurely, the Prees Branch tempts all but the most determinedly chaste of main line passers-by into exploration of its reedy, if foreshortened charms. No, you can no longer emulate the antics of that illustrious old boatman Jack (*Shropshire Union Fly-Boats*) Roberts and his father who, on shovelling eighteen tons of North Staffordshire coal from the hold of their boat *Times* at Edstaston Wharf on a hot June day in 1908, flung off their clothes and dived into the canal in a dual attempt to clean up and cool off.

Even that long ago, the branch was silting up; it had taken their horse two hours to drag the boat the last mile. Subsequently the far three miles were abandoned, navigable status remaining just as far as the 'clay hole' from whence much of the 'puddle' for lining the bed of the Ellesmere Canal emanated. Towards the

end of his working life in the 1960s, Jack was employed by British Waterways to convey Whixall clay to where it was required aboard the horse-drawn boat *Antwerp*. Latterly, the clay hole was developed into a marina which, to this day, offers a legitimate excuse for a detour up the arm, and a chance to negotiate its two charming timber lift-bridges.

Surprisingly, considering that the much larger town of Wem might have been a more profitable objective, the branch was intended to reach Prees but fell short by a couple of miles. Wharves were provided at Waterloo and Edstaston, together with a bank of lime burning kilns at Quina Brook; burnt lime being an important farming commodity in the innocent days before chemical fertilizers.

An unusual three-storey canal house

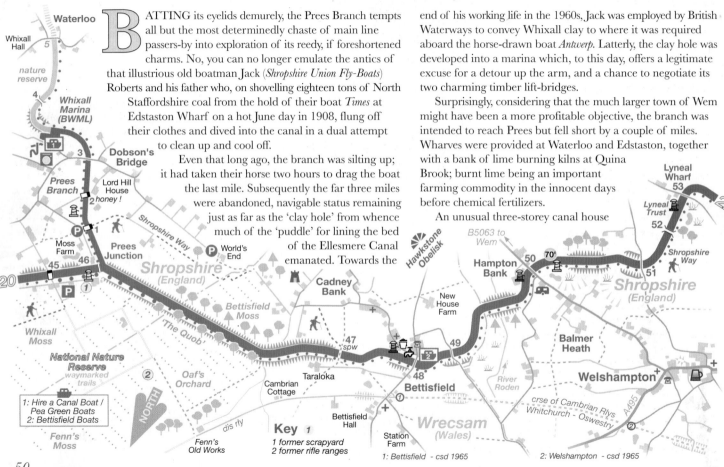

Waterloo
Whixall Hall
5
nature reserve
4
Whixall Marina (BWML)
3
Dobson's Bridge
Prees Branch
Lord Hill House
2 honey !
Moss Farm
Prees Junction
World's End
Shropshire Way
Shropshire (England)
45 46
Whixall Moss
National Nature Reserve
waymarked trails
1: Hire a Canal Boat / Pea Green Boats
2: Bettisfield Boats
Fenn's Moss
Oaf's Orchard
The Quob
Fenn's Old Works
dis rly
Bettisfield Moss
Cadney Bank
Taraloka
Cambrian Cottage
Bettisfield Hall
Station Farm
47 spw
48
Bettisfield
Wrecsam (Wales)
Hawkstone Obelisk
B5063 to Wem
New House Farm
49
River Roden
Hampton Bank
50 70'
51
Balmer Heath
Welshampton
crse of Cambrian Rlys
Whitchurch - Oswestry
A495
Lyneal Wharf
53
Lyneal Trust
52
Shropshire Way
Shropshire (England)
22
20

Key 1
1 former scrapyard
2 former rifle ranges

1: Bettisfield - csd 1965
2: Welshampton - csd 1965

NORTH

watches over Prees Junction, its ground floor lying below the level of the canal. West of the junction, a long straight mile, known colloquially as 'The Quob' - possibly because mires tend to quiver and throb when walked upon - extends across the mosses, evoking an aura every bit as eerie as its nickname. It was not an easy length of canal to cut. Drainage of the peat caused subsidence and the canal company employed a permanent Moss Gang responsible for raising oak-piled clay embankments. Similarly the railway builders, sixty years later, had to lay their track on rafts of faggots and larch poles. Progress rended the gang redundant when steel-piling was introduced in the 1960s, but you can still see how the towpath lies lower than the water, suggesting that instabilities in the landscape remain. A slender timber post, part of the Mosses Trail, marks the boundary between England and Wales, but the canal's familiarity with the latter is shortlived on this occasion, a mere taster of the splendours to come if you are travelling westbound.

Prees Branch, Bridge 1

Though there are no facilities as such, Bettisfield repays closer examination. Uphill to the north stands the quaintly Victorian church, designed by G. E. Street in 1874: the stone was quarried on Grinshill, the stained glass is by Clayton & Bell, the tiles Minton, the bells from Taylor's foundry in Loughborough. The buildings at Bettisfield's Beechinged station have at least derived tender loving care from their domestic occupants, the goods shed being an especially attractive conversion. Enigmatic crests adorn the rail-side parapets of the overbridge. The railway's trackbed can be explored in an easterly direction to the skeletal remains of a former peat works. A mile to the north, Bettisfield Park (or Hall), seat of the Hanmer family saw use as a military camp during both world wars, bringing many troop trains to the line. Taraloka - formerly a farmhouse called Cornhill - is a Buddhist retreat for women.

Hampton Bank is one of the Llangollen Canal's lesser sung engineering achievements; it carries the canal perhaps thirty feet above a headwater of the River Roden, a tributary of the Tern which joins the Severn below Shrewsbury. Larches mask the bank from the prevailing wind. To the south-east, beyond Wem, stands obelisk-topped Grotto Hill in Hawkstone Park; to the north-west the mountains of Wales. Hampton was another place where lime burning for agriculture took place. L. T. C. Rolt moored at Hampton aboard *Cressy* for a month in the summer of 1947, having been thwarted in an attempt to reach Pontcysyllte because of excessive weed and general decay in the canal beyond Ellesmere.

Prees Branch, Bridge 3

ENCHANTING Ellesmere embraces the canal which it once gave its name to with the enthusiasm of a doting aunt, a perfume-bosomed response to the commerce it continues to bring to the community coffers two centuries after its conception. Yes, it's worth recalling that what we know glibly as the Llangollen Canal is a term which would be unfamiliar to the canal's promoters. For historically this was the Ellesmere Canal, an ambitious attempt to link the rivers Mersey, Dee and Severn with a main line from Chester to Shrewsbury. In the event, only the Pontcysyllte-Weston Lullingfields section was ever built with, from Welsh Frankton (Map 23), branches to Llanymynech and Elles-mere itself. As it became apparent that

the intended main line of the canal would never reach the Dee or Severn, the Ellesmere Canal Company cut a canal eastwards from Ellesmere to meet the Chester Canal near Nantwich. Hurleston was reached in the year of Trafalgar: two things to celebrate!

Forty years later the Ellesmere Canal amalgamated with the Chester Canal and the new Birmingham & Liverpool Junction Canal to form the Shropshire Union Railways & Canal Company. The route from Hurleston to Llangollen was known as the 'Welsh Section'.

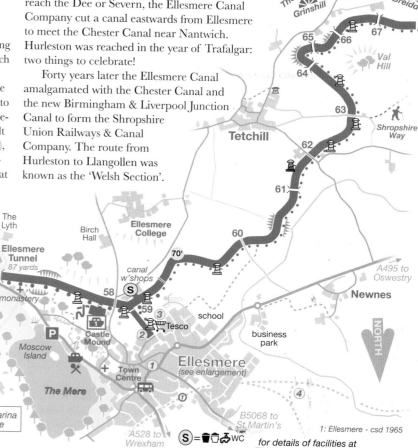

Key ①

1 former rennet works
2 canal warehouse
3 site of cheese factory
4 site of munitions dump

1: Blackwater Marina
ABC Boat Hire

1: Ellesmere - csd 1965

for details of facilities at
Ellesmere turn to page 54

The term 'Llangollen Canal' didn't gain general currency until the Canal & River Trust's nationalised predecessors, British Waterways, published a quaint little cruising guide under that title in 1956.

Ellesmere became the headquarters of the canal and the company built imposing offices here. Known as Beech House, these premises still preside over the canal junction, though used residentially for many years now, CRT being confined to the charmingly higgledy-piggledy maintenance base next door. Much of the infrastructure of this facility dates back to the earliest years of the canal. Particularly notable is the handsome stone drydock with distinctive weathervane in the shape of a narrowboat atop its slate roof. Workshops of timber and stone construction include a joiner's shop, blacksmith's forge and pattern store where wooden templates used for making accurate moulds for iron castings are kept; though, alas, rarely if ever used. Lock gate manufacture ceased at Ellesmere in 1961. An illuminating account of one man's working life at the yard appeared in *Narrow Boat* magazine's Winter 2011/12 issue.

Opposite Beech House a short arm leads to the town wharf. A relatively fresh addition to the canalscape here is the sculpture of an upturned boat, sweetly adorned inside with etched tiles. Just under the cast iron footbridge which spans the arm a boathouse stood at an oblique angle on the off-side. Of two stories, with a hay loft, it's exact significance has been lost in the mists of time, and it was regrettably demolished in 1951.

For most of its life the arm was overlooked by industrial premises that had originally been opened as an ironworks, but which later became a dairy. Now, new housing is steadily (though not exactly stealthily) encroaching, and together with a Tesco supermarket the feel is overtly suburban. In the midst of this transformation a Shropshire Union warehouse stands disorientated, like a pensioner attending a rave. It appears beyond the wit of Ellesmere to find a sustainable use for it; ditto their substantial railway station, also earmarked to be engulfed by a housing development.

East of Ellesmere the Llangollen Canal undertakes a hauntingly lovely journey through Shropshire's own 'lakeland'. There are seven lakes, or meres, in the neighbourhood of Ellesmere without inflow or outflow. They were formed at the end of the Ice Age, 10,000 years ago, as the great glaciers retreated and melted waters collected in cups of the land. The meres support a resident population of birds including kingfishers, herons, grebe, Canada geese, coots and moorhens. In winter there's an influx of wildfowl. On hot late summer evenings the phenomenon of 'breaking' occurs, as algae rise from the depths to spread a deep blue-green veil upon the surface. Cole Mere (used by a sailing club, and the only place in England where the rare Least Water Lily grows wild) and Blake Mere both lie beside the canal, the latter only separated from the waterway by a narrow belt of trees which provide shade for picnics on warm summer days. Forget the helter-skelter rush towards Llangollen, this is one of the true highlights of the canal, a place to linger, unwind and find a real sense of peace. The unique charm of the meres was evoked in Mary Webb's 1926 novel *Precious Bane*. The little Monastery of Our Lady & St Joseph by Ellesmere Tunnel is home to an order of Poor Clare Colettines.

Westwards, the canal rapidly escapes into empty countryside, skirting the playing fields of Ellesmere College, a Woodard boarding school, and the shop-less, pub-less village of Tetchill. The towpath has been designated as part of the Shropshire Way, though is not particularly well maintained. Val Hill sounds like a fourth-former you might have been so smitten with as to etch her name on your pencil case. But in fact it's a tree-topped glacial mound picturesquely forcing the canal into an extra bend or two on its way to Welsh Frankton. Workmen, mending a fence on the slopes of the hill in the 1890s, uncovered a Bronze Age sword in two halves, obligingly reunited for posterity by the local black-smith. Would that he was still around to reunite the broken pieces of the Montgomery Canal.

A public footpath (part of the Shropshire Way) leads from Bridge 63 to Welsh Frankton more directly than the canal. It is a pity that it doesn't cross the summit of Val Hill, because the views from there must be terrific. As it is, even from the canal you can see Grinshill in the middle distance to the south-east and - in clear conditions - much further away in reduced chromatic tones, the A. E. Housmanesque outlines of The Wrekin, Clee Hills, Wenlock Edge; the Caradocs and the Long Mynd.

Ellesmere

Map 22

Ellesmere is an increasingly rare find: a small, unspoilt country town with no pretensions. Life seems as slowly lived here as the rhythmic lapping of waters on the shores of the meres. Visitors - whether they come by car to feed the ducks, or by boat along the Llangollen Canal - are assimilated without the usual symptomatic rash of tourist paraphernalia. The local economy has traditionally been an agricultural one, though in the past there was an ironworks, an important railway junction, canal workshops and a rennet factory. Worryingly, like resting thespians, some of these buildings are in need of new roles and the local powers that be seem reluctant or clueless how to achieve this. But what the visitor sees today is a late 19th century country town preserved almost in aspic, and all very endearing it is too.

There is so much to see and do that only CRT's time limits curtail an increasing desire to stay put. Early risers get the town and its environs to themselves and can walk into the past with impunity. Go and pay homage to the substantial old railway station before it is subsumed by new housing. Here the station master John Hood was sacked in 1892 for standing up to the Cambrian Railways unfair dismissal of a porter. Questions were raised in Parliament and Ellesmere's inhabitants collected enough money for Hood to buy a house which he lived in until he died, never rejoining the railway.

If your inclination is for more rural climes, take the path which leaves the towpath half way between Ellesmere Tunnel and Bridge 58. It leads to woodland cared for by the Shropshire Wildlife Trust which was used for allotments during the Second World War. Thence you can find your way to The Mere before the rest of the world has woken up. How nice to have it to yourself!

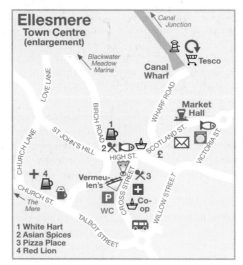

Ellesmere Town Centre (enlargement)

1 White Hart
2 Asian Spices
3 Pizza Place
4 Red Lion

Eating & Drinking

ASIAN SPICES - Birch Road. Tel: 01691 623689. Indian restaurant and take-away (ex Mon). SY12 0ET
THE BOAT HOUSE - Mereside. Tel: 01691 623852. Cafe/bistro in picturesque waterside setting. Open daily from 8.30am for breakfasts, coffees, lunches and teas. Evening meals from 6pm on Fri & Sat. SY12 0PA
THE PIZZA PLACE - Cross Street. Tel: 01691 623772. Open Tue-Sat from 5pm plus Sat 12-3pm. SY12 0AY
RED LION - Church Street. Tel: 01691 622632. Friendly Thwaites pub en route to mere for generously portioned mixed grills etc. SY12 0HD
WHITE HART - Birch Road. Tel: 01691 624653. *Good Beer Guide* listed half-timbered ale house specialising in for the most part locally sourced beers. SY12 0ET
There are two fish & chip shops, and plenty of additional tea rooms and takeaways as befits a tourist destination.

Shopping

A substantial Tesco supermarket overlooks the canal wharf, absolving shoppers of any real need to patronise the town's traditional retailers. But to venture no further would represent a failure of responsibility and a lost opportunity, for Ellesmere boasts some fine independent shops, the acme of which is Vermeulen's delicatessen on Cross Street (Tel: 01691 622521) by the town square. Their pork pies - often still warm to the touch by mid-morning - hold a permanent place in our Top Six Purveyors of Pork Pies Accessible by Inland Waterway Awards*, whilst the cold counter contains a mouthwatering array of glazed meats, pates, shellfish and cheeses. Get them to grind some coffee beans for you then dare yourself to leave without a box of their fresh cream cakes.

The indoor market, housed in a handsome Victorian pile opposite the post office, operates on Tuesdays. Thursday is half day. There are several banks in the town and a launderette on Victoria Street.

Self-Catering

ABC offer self-catering for up to six people in an appartment at Blackwater Marina - Tel: 0330 333 0590.

Connections

BUSES - Arriva service 53 runs to/from Oswestry at 40 minute intervals (ex Sun) and in doing so provides a link with the nearest railhead at Gobowen. Towpath walkers may like to note that it crosses the canal at Bridge 13w, Map 24. Tanat Valley 449 also runs to/from Oswestry, but via Whittington, crossing the canal at Bridge 5w Map 23. GHA 501 connects Ellesmere with Shrewsbury. Tel: 0871 200 2233.

TAXIS - Oswestry Cabs. Tel: 01691 881000.

*The other five are currently: Eastwood's of Berkhamsted; Grange's of Slaithwaite; McArdle's of Chirk; Mitchell's of Huddersfield; and Webb's of Northwich.

Images of
Ellesmere

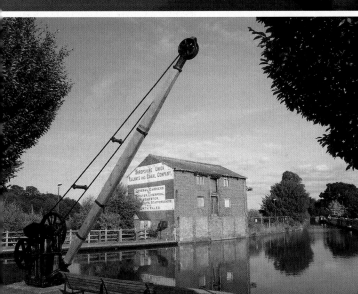

OUT in the middle of the middle of nowhere, Welsh Frankton, or Frankton Junction, was the hub of the Ellesmere canal system. From two junctions in the form of an H, routes radiated to Pontcysyllte, Ellesmere, Weston Lullingfields (the intended main line to Shrewsbury) and Llanymynech. The canal continued onwards from there as the Montgomeryshire Canal through Welshpool to Newtown. This route, amounting to some 35 miles, is now known as the Montgomery Canal. In 1936 a breach occurred where the canal crossed the River Perry by aqueduct (Map 27) and the LMS Railway, who owned the canal, chose not to repair it, stranding the last carrier, George Beck, in the process. Eight years later the canal was legally abandoned. In the ensuing fifty years the Montgomery Canal might well have decayed irredeemably had not its scenic splendour been recognised as the canals underwent a revival for pleasure use. Frankton Locks were restored in 1987 but stood idle for almost ten years, until a further restoration project, involving construction of a new lock -

named after Graham Palmer, founder of the heroic Waterway Recovery Group - allowed boats to reach Perry Aqueduct. A new brick and steel aqueduct was subsequently built to replace the previous stone structure and the first section of the canal is now navigable for seven miles to Gronwen Wharf. Indeed, over half the waterway's thirty-five miles have been restored, as described in the text accompanying Maps 27 to 34.

The canalscape at Frankton is typically self-effacing. Pretty enough with its lock flight, but it's not until you begin to poke about a bit that fragments of the past percolate through. No sign

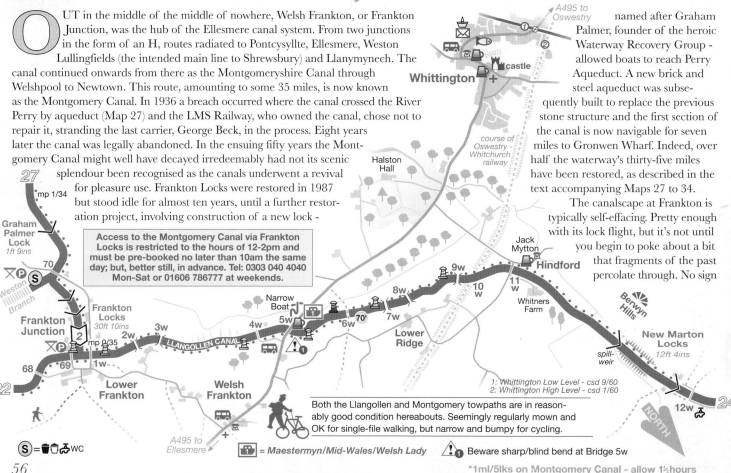

Access to the Montgomery Canal via Frankton Locks is restricted to the hours of 12-2pm and must be pre-booked no later than 10am the same day; but, better still, in advance. Tel: 0303 040 4040 Mon-Sat or 01606 786777 at weekends.

1: Whittington Low Level - csd 9/60
2: Whittington High Level - csd 1/60

Both the Llangollen and Montgomery towpaths are in reasonably good condition hereabouts. Seemingly regularly mown and OK for single-file walking, but narrow and bumpy for cycling.

(S) = 🗑🧺♿WC

🖼 = *Maestermyn/Mid-Wales/Welsh Lady*   ⚠1 Beware sharp/blind bend at Bridge 5w

*1ml/5lks on Montgomery Canal - allow 1½hours

of the warehouse and crane which stood where cars now park by Bridge 69; no toll clerk in the check house by the top chamber; no banter from the Canal Tavern at the foot of the staircase, though the curious steps and an iron bar are tangible reminders. A plaque at the tail of the third lock down recalls that L. T. C. Rolt's *Cressy* was converted into a leisure craft at Beech's boat dock in 1929; the dock and workshops lined the lock. *Cressy* had been purchased by an uncle of Rolt's from Peates Mill (see Map 28), having originally been built by the Shropshire Union Canal Carrying Company at Trevor during the First World War.

Frankton Junction

As well as adding extra accommodation, Beech's installed a vertical compound steam engine, for hitherto *Cressy* had been horse-drawn. Rolt accompanied his uncle on the refurbished boat's maiden voyage to Barlaston, on the Trent & Mersey south of Stoke-on-Trent, one misty morning in March 1930. With such memories to assimilate, Frankton makes a good spot to moor overnight. It is not only activity on the canal that has vanished: up the lane the former Free Church chapel of 1890 stands strangled by trees.

Meanwhile, the Llangollen Canal - whose bridge numbers begin again at '1', albeit with the recently appended suffix 'w' (just in case you thought you'd dozed off and assumed you were back at Hurleston!) - traverses a low shelf above the valley of the Perry. The Berwyn and Breidden hills of the Border Marches rise up in the west; benignly blue or intimidatingly black according to weather conditions. At Hindford the Cambrian Railways line crosses the canal again (or at least it did until 1965) and the Vyrnwy Aqueduct passes invisibly beneath the canal, conveying water supplies to Liverpool.

Not least for its congenial pub, Hindford is another nice place to moor overnight. At the T junction an old signpost points intriguingly to a place called "Iron Mills". Nearby Halston Hall owes much of its architecture to Robert Mylne (of whom more on Map 27) and was the home of John 'Mad Jack' Mytton who was born at Halston with a silver spoon in his mouth in 1797, but died in a debtor's prison thirty seven years later. During a brief life largely devoted to debauchery, he was in the habit of holding up departing guests on the Oswestry road in the guise of a highwayman.

New Marton locks provide the boater with some not unwelcome exercise, though they can be as prone to queues as Grindley Brook when they have a mind to be. Westbound they are the last to be encountered; eastbound it is some twenty miles to the next one: so be inclined to take delays in your stride. We bumped into some uncharacteristically humble Australians, chastened that their cricketers were ineptly losing the Ashes.

57

24 LLANGOLLEN CANAL Chirk (Y Waun) 5mls/0lks/2½hrs

SHROPSHIRE'S soft farmlands give way to the rugged mountains of Wales. Well, at least if you're journeying westwards they do. Not that eastbound travellers must brace themselves for an anti-climax. On the contrary, the Llangollen Canal keeps delightful surprises up its sleeve whichever direction you are going in.

St Martin's Moor is low-lying and cross-hatched by drainage dykes. On the horizon to the north stands St Martin's 13th century parish church. Its substantial tower reminded Michael Moulder of the Cotswolds in his 1973 Shell Guide. A far cry from Coventry Cathedral, the village's school was designed by Basil Spence in the 1950s. Though part of the Denbighshire coalfield, Ifton Colliery (1913-68) was the largest in Shropshire, employing thirteen hundred men in its heyday. The mineral line from the pit head to the exchange sidings at Weston Rhyn was steeply graded, and trains officially limited to ten loaded wagons. Imagine the din as one of the mine's internal Hudswell Clarke tank engines, *Richboro* (formerly of a dock on the Kent coast) or *Unity*, crossed the

the canal at Rhoswiel on the ferocious ascent to the main line.

Beyond Bridge 13w (where one or two buildings betray their canal heritage) the countryside becomes hilly and wooded. Two extensive country properties have experienced different fates: Henlle Hall is a holiday centre and golf course; Moreton Hall a girls school whose playing fields border the canal. As the canal approaches Chirk it passes the sites of a number of long forgotten basins linked to early coal mines (Preesgwyn, Trehowell, Quinta et al) by primitive tramways. A marshy field betrays scant remains of Gledrid Wharf where the originally horse-drawn Glyn Valley Tramway

Key ①

1 site of Ifton Colliery
2 sites of misc. wharves
3 sites of misc. old colys.
4 site of Gledrid Wharf (GVT)
5 site of brickworks
6 site of transhipment basin

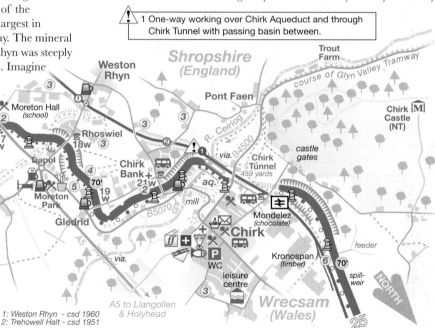

⚠ 1 One-way working over Chirk Aqueduct and through Chirk Tunnel with passing basin between.

1: Weston Rhyn - csd 1960
2: Trehowell Halt - csd 1951

connected with the canal prior to being converted to steam haulage and redirected to Chirk. At Bridge 19w the canal assumes World Heritage Site status all the way through to Horseshoe Falls (Map 26). A well-produced handbook, written by Peter Wakelin and published by the Canal & River Trust and Royal Commission on the Ancient & Historical Monuments of Wales, is obtainable from Trevor Basin Visitor Centre.

Chirk Bank was a busy canal centre up until the 1920s. Employed on maintenance duties in the 1950s, Jack Roberts (q.v.) was housed in one of the aqueduct cottages, and British Waterways built him a small stable for his boat horse from corrugated iron which still stands. His wife, however, didn't take to Chirk Bank, because the high trees on the offside meant that the house received hardly any sunshine.

British border crossings don't come much more dramatic than the canal's entry into Chirk. Only the Royal Border Bridge at Berwick can match the excitement of crossing from England to Wales (or vice versa) seventy feet up in the air above the rushing River Ceiriog. Solely the fact that you no longer arrive in Denbighshire subtracts from the magic.

The original conception for an aqueduct at Chirk was that it would span the valley downstream of its present site, and that it should consist of a relatively short iron span approached on either side by lofty embankments. But the Myddeltons of Chirk Castle (*nimbys* with clout) took umbrage at what they considered would be a despoliation of their view and persuaded the canal company to think again. In the event the Chirk Aqueduct unveiled in 1801 consisted of an iron trough carried upon ten

Bridging the border, Chirk

masonry arches. As such it represents a half-way house between the first generation of canal aqueducts, which held the water in a bed of puddled clay, and the dizzy achievement of nearby Pontcysyllte, where the iron trough was allowed to fly free from its masonry fetters. Widely accepted as a romantic addition to the landscape, the aqueduct spanned the Ceiriog valley in splendid isolation for the best part of half a century until a railway arrived on the scene. We used, blithely, to inform Canal Companion users that the watercolourist John Sell Cotman had painted a view of the aqueduct in all its early glory. Indeed, it was believed he had, and it hung in the Victoria & Albert Museum, only for an art historian to declare that the subject was Crambe Beck Bridge near Kirkham in Yorkshire on the road from York to Malton. The past, like a fresh-faced, corduroy-jacketed graduate teacher, marching into class eager to redefine the syllabus, is always rewriting itself.

Delivering the coal, Rhoswiel

Completed in 1848, for the Shrewsbury & Chester Railway - which became part of the GWR's main line from Paddington to Birkenhead - construction of a rival structure in such close proximity might have been expected to mar the impact of the aqueduct, but in fact the second bridge only served to enhance the setting and drama of the first. From whichever angle you consider their juxtaposition, these two great structures seem to form an homogeneous whole and share such a unity within the landscape that the border would now be inconceivable and less dramatic without

them. At the north end of the aqueduct a broad pool (where boats frequently jostle while waiting for the aqueduct or tunnel to clear) leads to Chirk Tunnel, 459 yards long with a cantilevered towpath running through; with typical altruism, Telford considered the hitherto established practice of 'legging' by boatmen to be dangerous and undignified.

Beyond the northern portal of Chirk Tunnel the canal penetrates a wooded cutting of some magnitude; there are visitor moorings here but not much in the way of television or mobile phone reception. At its far end a winding hole marks the site of a former transhipment wharf between the canal, the collieries at Black Park and Brynkinhalt, and the narrow gauge Glyn Valley Tramway. What a loss this charming narrow gauge line became when competition from lorries and buses precipitated its downfall in 1935. Built to serve mines and quarries at the head of the Ceiriog Valley, it also carried passengers. In *Landscape With Machines*, L. T. C. Rolt describes 'swaying and rattling down a steep gradient through thick woods to the floor of the valley at Pontfaen' on visits to his uncle at Glynceiriog. Perhaps the experience may one day be repeatable, for two separate groups have enthusiastic ambitions of resurrecting the GVT, initially through interpretation, but eventually by re-laying as much of the track as feasible. Clearing parties are already at work and you may see signs of such activity in the vicinity.

Whittington
Map 23

A village - chiefly remarkable for its picturesque castle remains - situated two miles west of the canal on what used to be the A5 London-Holyhead road. The substantial red brick 18th century church is notable for its tracery and Jesse window.

Eating & Drinking
NARROWBOAT INN - canalside Bridge 5w, Tel: 01691 661051. Cosy little pub purpose-built by the adjoining boatyard. SY11 4NU
Two other pubs and fish & chips in village centre.

Shopping
Post office stores in village centre.

Things to Do
WHITTINGTON CASTLE - Tel: 01691 662500. Largely just the gatehouse remains of this 13th century castle, unusually under the care of the local community! Open 10am-4pm Wed to Sun in summer (Fri-Sun in winter). Tea room and shop. SY11 4DF

Connections
BUSES - Tanat Valley service 449 operates hourly, Mon-Sat to/from Ellesmere and Oswestry (there is a stop beside the Narrowboat Inn at Bridge 5w). Tel: 0871 200 2233.

Hindford
Map 23

JACK MYTTON - adjacent Bridge 11w. Tel: 01691 679861. Country inn which derives its name from the eccentric 19th century squire of nearby Halston Hall. Steaks and burgers, grills, salads and vegetarian dishes. Local ales. SY11 4NL

Chirk
Map 24

Anxious to push on to Pontcysyllte, many boaters do not bother to visit Chirk. Their loss, because the village centre contains an interesting selection of buildings, including the parish church of St Mary's (whose double-aisled interior has the air of a small cathedral); the remains of a motte and bailey castle; and a war memorial of Portland stone carved by sculptor and typographer Eric Gill. Look out for the wrought iron sculpture depicting a boat and train on the bridges on the park gate opposite, and the plaque commemorating Billy Meredith, born here in 1874, the 'wing wizard' who won the Welsh Cup with Chirk FC and went on to play for both Manchester clubs and his country on many occasions. Once almost exclusively a mining community, Chirk is now dominated by the Mondelez (formerly Cadbury) hot chocolate factory and the adjoining Kronospan timber works which receives incoming raw timber by train from the company's own plantations in Scotland and Devon. Still on a railway theme, Dapol, the model railway company, have their headquarters (and a shop) on the industrial estate at Gledrid.

Eating & Drinking
THE BOATHOUSE - Tel: 01691 772493. A wide selection of traditional food 11am-2.30pm/5.30-9pm Mon-Sat. Access via marina (Map 25). LL14 5AD
BRIDGE INN - Tel: 01691 773213. 'Last pub in England' just down from Bridge 21w. LL14 5BU
CAFFI WYLFA - Castle Road. Tel: 01691 770492. Friendly community run cafe open 10am-5pm daily (sometimes later in summer). LL14 5BS
THE CHIRK TANDOORI - Station Avenue. Tel: 01691 772499. Village centre Indian. LL14 5LU
THE HAND HOTEL - Church Street. Tel: 01691 773472. Coaching inn which has long been catering for travellers on Telford's Holyhead road. Bar and restaurant food. Accommodation. LL14 5EY
LION QUAYS - canalside Bridge 17w. Tel: 01691 684300. Hotel and conference centre thoughtfully providing 'herring-bone' mooring pontoons for boating patrons. SY11 3EN

LORD MORETON - Tel: 01691 778888. Bar/restaurant, part of the Moreton Park complex best reached from Bridge 19w. LL14 5DG
THE POACHERS - canalside Bridge 19w. Tel: 01691 773250. Marston's 'Rotisserie' all-day pub with moorings outside. LL14 5DG
PLOUGH INN - Station Road, Weston Rhyn. Tel: 01691 772536. Village local about half a mile's walk west from Bridge 18w. SY10 7SX

Shopping
Make a B-line for McArdle's butchers and their wide range of locally sourced produce; they also do delicious take-away hot roast baps, pies etc: their pork pies are exceptional! The village also supports a baker, grocer, pharmacy, Spar and a branch of the HSBC Bank. Wyedale's Moreton Park garden centre (accessed via Bridge 19w) offers a wide range of shopping opportunities, including a well-stocked farm shop. Chirk Trout Farm lies about a mile west of the canal on the B4500. Open Mon-Fri 9am-5pm and Sat 10am to 4pm, they sell their own fish produce together with cheese, eggs, pies and cakes and postcards of the GVT.

Things to Do
CHIRK CASTLE - Just over a mile from the north end of the tunnel. Tel: 01691 777701. Over seven hundred years of history and continual habitation to soak up. Open March-October, Wed-Sun, 10am-6pm. National Trust shop, restaurant. Admission charge. LL14 5AF

Connections
BUSES - Bryn Melyn service 64 bi-hourly Mon-Sat to/from Llangollen (via Froncysyllte) and Glyn Ceiriog. Arriva services 2/2A to/from Oswestry and Wrexham half-hourly Mon-Sat, hourly Sun. Tel: 0871 200 2233.
TRAINS - Arriva Trains Wales services to/from Chester and Holyhead and Shrewsbury, Cardiff and Birmingham. Tel: 03457 484950.
TAXIS - B&L: Tel: 01691 776444.

25 LLANGOLLEN CANAL Pontcysyllte & Trevor 5½ mls/0lks/2½hrs

WHITEHOUSES Tunnel ushers the canal into Offa's Dyke country, and the towpath is suddenly swollen by walkers on the long distance footpath of that name. Boater and walker alike are treated to an enchanted passage through a mask of woodland on a shelf above the River Dee. Given the right conditions, the delicious aroma of pinewood fills the air. Between the ivy clad boles of the tall trees there are glimpses of an impressive railway viaduct. Like the canal builders before them, the railway engineers had to respond to the challenge of the Dee's deep valley. A goods railway paralleled the canal, initially on the topwath side, before passing beneath the canal via a stone-built aqueduct; traces of the turntables, laboriously employed to manhandle wagons through right-angles may still be discerned. On the outskirts of Froncysyllte the lofty former Pen-y-Graig limekilns recall lost industry alongside the canal. Negotiating lift-bridge 28w, the canal approaches its climax on a huge embankment built from spoil excavated when Chirk Tunnel was dug.

Superlatives are superfluous when it comes to describing Pontcysyllte Aqueduct, which carries the canal one hundred and twenty feet high

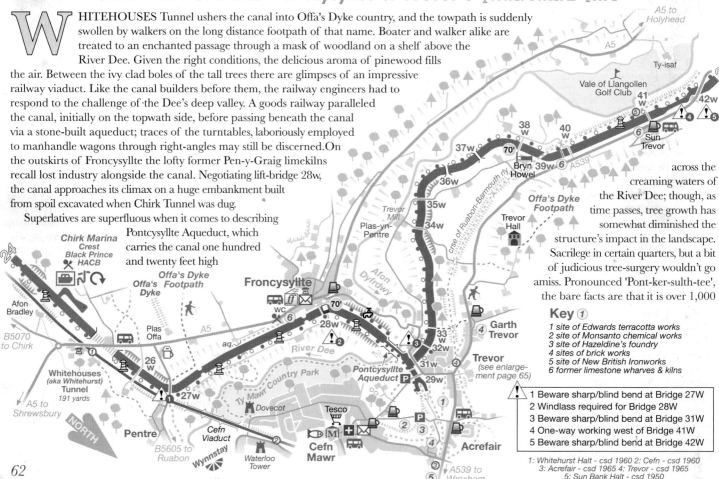

across the creaming waters of the River Dee; though, as time passes, tree growth has somewhat diminished the structure's impact in the landscape. Sacrilege in certain quarters, but a bit of judicious tree-surgery wouldn't go amiss. Pronounced 'Pont-ker-sulth-tee', the bare facts are that it is over 1,000

Key ①

1 site of Edwards terracotta works
2 site of Monsanto chemical works
3 site of Hazeldine's foundry
4 sites of brick works
5 site of New British Ironworks
6 former limestone wharves & kilns

⚠ 1 Beware sharp/blind bend at Bridge 27W
2 Windlass required for Bridge 28W
3 Beware sharp/blind bend at Bridge 31W
4 One-way working west of Bridge 41W
5 Beware sharp/blind bend at Bridge 42W

1: Whitehurst Halt - csd 1960 2: Cefn - csd 1960
3: Acrefair - csd 1965 4: Trevor - csd 1965
5: Sun Bank Halt - csd 1950

feet long, 127 feet tall at its deepest point, and consists of an iron trough supported by 18 stone piers. The aqueduct was completed in 1805, the year of Nelson's death at Trafalgar. Four hundred and fifty-eight 'Englishmen' perished at Trafalgar, but only one life was lost in construction of the aqueduct; a misfortune attributed to a moment of carelessness.

Along with the Menai Suspension Bridge, Pontcysyllte used to be ranked among Telford's outstanding achievements, but in his last book, *Thomas Telford's Temptation* (M&M Baldwin 1993), the eminent canal historian, Charles Hadfield, felt that posterity had emphasised Telford's contribution at the expense of William Jessop's; the latter being, after all, the Ellesmere Canal Company's Engineer, whereas Telford was merely its General Agent. Didn't we caution you about the past on the previous map? Personally, we'd be loathe to traduce Telford: perish the thought that one day all Mr Pearson's hard work might be reattributed to Mr Nicholson. Whoever you prefer to credit, this remarkable act of civil engineering was contemporaneously dubbed 'the stream in the sky', and fulfils that description in the minds of awestruck tourists to this day. Incidentally, just as Chirk Aqueduct finally materialised in a somewhat different form to that initially conceived, so, early in its conception, it was suggested that Pontcysyllte be erected at a lower height, reached, at either end by a flight of locks, though Jessop quickly realised that this would create severe water supply difficulties.

Boaters are likely to be too intoxicated with the notion that their vessel has suddenly taken flight to be concerned with the far horizon. But pedestrians, the numbers of which have exponentially increased with Pontcysyllte's lately acquired celebrity status, have time to savour the panoramic views the aqueduct engenders: westwards up the Vale of Llangollen; eastwards to the purlieus of Wynnstay, former seat of the Williams Wynn family who once owned so many estates in Wales and neighbouring Shropshire that they were dubbed the 'Kings of Wales'. Their parkland was laid out by Capability Brown and the lofty column you can just about pick out celebrates the 4th Baronet who died in 1789, an influential patron of the arts who had his portrait painted by Joshua Reynolds and his London town house designed by Robert Adam.

From Trevor, the canal was to have carried on over the neighbouring ridge and then down through Wrexham to the Dee at Chester. Such a course would have required many locks, a very long tunnel or a series of boat lifts. The enormity of this undertaking, coupled with the recession which occurred as an aftermath to the Napoleonic Wars, thwarted the Ellesmere Canal Company's plans to provide a direct canal between the Mersey and the Severn. Doubtless the terrain could have been overcome in time, but the outlay involved would have broken the bank.

In place of the envisaged main line northwards, the canal beyond the aqueduct passed through Bridge 29w and terminated at a twin-armed transhipment wharf from where, first a tramway, then later a railway (some of whose rails are still, enigmatically in place), connected with quarries and collieries on the higher ground towards Ruabon. A further arm - known as the Plas Kynaston Canal - described an arc to the east serving chemical, terracotta and iron works in the vicinity. It was at Plas Kynaston that the ironmaster, William Hazeldine, cast the arches and trough for Pontcysyllte Aqueduct. In the Ellesmere Canal's commercial heyday much traffic was generated in the neighbourhood. Trefynant Fireclay Works was one of the most notable industries. Owned by James Coster Edwards, the business grew to merit being described as the 'largest and most successful manufacturer of terracotta in the world'. On the back of such success, Edwards erected a mansion for himself beside the canal at Bryn Howel which is now an hotel adjacent to Bridge 38w. The works closed in 1965, but you can still pay homage to the entrance gates - decorated with terracotta, naturally - on Llangollen Road, the A539.

A canal to Llangollen was not originally planned. Only when it became clear that the main line would never be completed did the company decide to provide a feeder from the River Dee at Llantysilio to the canal at Trevor. The cutting of a canal along the steep slopes of the Vale of Llangollen

The towpath has been surfaced throughout the World Heritage Site, i.e. all the way from Bridge 19w at Gledrid (Map 24) to Horseshoe Falls (Map 26) and is thus in excelllent condition for walking and cycling alike.

'Stream in the Sky'

posed considerable problems and this was the last section of the canal to be completed, over two years after the aqueduct had been opened to traffic. This unforseen waterway is, not without irony therefore, widely recognised as one of the most scintillating lengths of canal in the country.

Moving off the aqueduct onto the feeder, or vice versa, boaters are forced to employ their best turning skills, often to an audience as ready to nit-pick as the judges on *Great British Bake Off.* All but the shortest boats are best advised to do it in at least two turns. A quick sequence of three overbridges ensues, thence the canal/feeder, call it what you will, essays a beguiling hillside course above the precipitous valley of the Dee. By Bridge 34w there are views down to the rooftops of Plas-yn-Pentre and its watermill on the riverbank. On the opposite side, Trevor Hall flaunts its Grade I listed richness. Dating from 1742, it can be hired for ludicrous sums of money. Between bridges 37w and 38w (how tedious this 'W' business becomes) there were wharves on the offside for limestone brought down from the surrounding hills by tramway. Canalside, at the Bryn Howel Hotel, is a half-timber gabled boathouse built by James Coster Edwards to keep a pleasure boat in. A delightful picture of a teak slipper launch rubbing shoulders with limestone narrowboats springs to mind.

Bridge 39w carried the Ruabon-Barmouth railway over the canal as it draws alongside the busy A539 Wrexham-Llangollen road. There were more limestone wharves between here and Sun Trevor. Unsurprisingly, given its precarious mountainside setting, the section between Trevor and Llangollen has a history of breaches. In 1945 the bank collapsed by Bridge 41w and the adjoining railway was swept away. Before any warning could be given, a goods train plunged into the gap and the driver was killed. Bursts occurred more frequently thereafter and by the mid nineteen-eighties it became apparent to British Waterways that this section would, effectively, have to be rebuilt. Nowadays the canal bed is concrete-lined, under-drained and fitted with a waterproof membrane.

'One Way Working'

Berwyn Boat Horse

Froncysyllte　　　　Map 25

A mountain goat of a village famed for its male voice choir who have gained a reputation as recording stars in recent years though (whisper it gently) they rehearse across the Dee in Acrefair. If your legs are up to it, it's worth following the zigzagging lane up to the crest of the ridge for spectacular views across the Dee Valley and up into the Vale of Llangollen; with, perhaps, a lusty rendition of *Men of Harlech* upon reaching the summit.

Dorothy Hartley, the social historian, lived at Fron House (overlooking Bridge 28w) from 1933 until her death at the age of 92 in 1985. *Food in England* was arguably her best known book, and it is still much revered, but a companion piece of perhaps more appeal to canallers was entitled *Water in England*. During the currency of the previous edition of this guide, teas and coffees had been available in the garden, but when we last passed by the property was For Sale. Dorothy's devotees - of which there are increasingly, not to say, belatedly many - can make a pilgrimage to her grave in St David's churchyard.

Eating & Drinking
AQUEDUCT INN - Holyhead Road. Tel: 01691 777118. You can't miss this *Good Beer Guide* listed free house standing high above the canal in its lemon sherbet paintwork. Local beers (including Stonehouse from Oswestry) bar food and good views over the aqueduct's approaches. LL20 7PY.
Also an Indian takeaway (Tel: 01691 774858) and Limekilns roadside cafe (open 7am-8pm daily) on the A5.

Shopping
Small post office stores on A5.

Connections
BUSES - Bryn Melyn service 64 Mon-Sat to/from Llangollen and Chirk. Tel: 0871 200 2233.

Trevor Basin (enlargement)

Trevor/Cefn Mawr　　　Map 25

Male voice choirs and villages (Rhosymedre, Gresford et al) that have given their names to well-loved hymns, where else could we be but Wales! The basin is hard by a housing estate, but the canal shrugs off such intrusions and a car park (with overspill) reflects the ever increasing popularity of the aqueduct.

Eating & Drinking
TELFORD INN - Tel: 01978 820469. Canalside pub formerly known as Scotch Hall, home to the canal's supervising engineer, Telford being a frequent visitor. Canalside adjoining the Anglo Welsh base. LL20 7TT
Refreshment kiosk at basin, and cafe at Jones the Boats.

Holiday Lets
DOCK HOUSE - Tel: 0117 304 1122. Self-catering for up to five persons at Trevor canal wharf. LL20 7TX

Shopping
The Premier convenience store (some 200 yards west of the canal basin) is open 7am-10pm daily. Cefn Mawr - pronounced as something vaguely like 'Kevin Mow' (the mow to rhyme with cow) boasts a large Tesco half a mile east of the canal basin.

Things to Do
TREVOR BASIN - Tel: 01978 822912. Visitor centre located by north end of Pontcysyllte. Displays concerning the construction of the aqueduct. Open daily Easter to October (weekends only in winter).
TRIP BOATS - Jones the Boats (Tel: 01978 824166) and Aqueduct Cruises (Tel: 01978 860702) both offer regular vertigo-defying cruises across the aqueduct.

Connections
BUSES - Arriva service 5 every 20 minutes (Mon-Sat) hourly (Sun) to/from Llangollen and Wrexham (via Ruabon railhead) from stops on the A539 at the north end of Station Road. Tel: 0871 200 2233.
BICYCLE HIRE - Cycles 2 Go. Tel: 01691 773532.

HAVING reached a crescendo at Pontcysyllte, the Llangollen Canal needs little encouragement to provide an encore, and treats you to all the wild majesty that the celebrated Vale of Llangollen can muster. Great buttresses of limestone cliffs tower above conifer plantations, making memories of Hurleston and gentle green Cheshire seem like something that occurred to someone else in another lifetime. When the weather is kind, you find yourself constantly lifting your eyes up into the hills, where sunlight gives the heather-clad ridges the clarity of well-executed marquetry. But Wales wouldn't be Wales if it weren't for the frequent, dripping Celtic mists that come creeping up the valley of the Dee, muffling boat exhausts and dampening the woods, though manifestly not the spirits.

Never exactly wide, the canal/feeder narrows as it approaches Llangollen with 'one way working' along three short sections cut through solid rock. Boaters need to be patient in high season, and a good deal of frustration can be saved simply by sending a member of your party (preferably the most diplomatic) ahead to check if a boat is approaching in the opposite direction. Linear visitor moorings are provided on the approach to Bridge 45w, but you may prefer (we do) to continue to the basin beyond where pontoons can accommodate over thirty boats. Whichever you decide on, you can stay for up to four hours free of charge as long as you depart no later than 5pm. Overnight stays of up to 24 hours cost £6; 48 hours £12, irrespective of the length of your boat.

1 Beware narrows west of here.
2 No powered boats beyond this point.

Fron Bache

Llangollen
(see enlargement)

Geraint Hill

Plas Newydd M

Town Centre

Eisteddfod Ground

70'

45w

46w

Geufron

47w

Llangollen Railway

Berwyn

Plas Berwyn

Horseshoe Falls

Llantysilio Hall

49w

WC

48Aw

NORTH

River Dee

A5

A539

44w

Wern Isaf

25 43w

Llandyn Hall

Castell Dinas Bran

Dinbren Hall

M

48w Motor Museum

aq.

Pentrefelin

River Dee

Valle Crucis Abbey M

A542 to Ruthin

S = WC

Berwyn Station

Chain Bridge

Horseshoe Falls

This, however, seems a small expenditure because each berth - be it linear alongside the towpath east of Llangollen Wharf, or in the mooring basin west of Bridge 45w - is equipped with water and electricity supplies. We've often said that other towns should be encouraged to provide similar secure and facility equipped berths for a small charge. Bear in mind though, that moorings at so popular a destination as this can be at a premium at the height of the season, and the earlier in the day you arrive, the more chance you'll have of finding a space.

Running above the slate roofs and salt-glazed chimney pots of the town the canal reaches the old Llangollen Wharf where the warehouse serves as a base for the horse-drawn boats which have been plying the final, narrow, shallow, transparent section up to Berwyn and the Chain Bridge since 1884. Powered boats are prohibited from proceeding beyond the mooring basin (opposite the Eisteddfod Ground) where, in any case, you will need to go to turn.

The feeder canal continues for another couple of miles beyond Llangollen to Llantysilio, an enchanting journey by any standards. Skirting the Eisteddfod Ground it passes beneath the main road to Ruthin before reaching Pentrefelin (Bridge 48w) where a former slate mill - served by a tramway which crossed the canal via a lift-bridge - now houses a fascinating display of motoring memorabilia and vehicles, including a nostalgic

recreation of a 1950s garage. Eglwyseg Aqueduct follows, parenthesised by a curving causeway. Beyond Ty Craig Bridge (48Aw) the canal is cut into the rock. Soon boat horses reach the limit of their exertions beside the Chain Bridge Hotel. The eponymous suspension bridge was re-opened in 2015 after a long period of disuse and provides a delightful means of reaching the Llangollen Railway's Berwyn station perched high above the Dee.

More of a viaduct, really, Kings Bridge (49w) dates from 1906 and was named in honour of Edward VII, its portal ushers you through to the last stretch of the feeder, the gauge house which controls the amount of water fed into the canal, and the massive, crescent-shaped Horseshoe Falls themselves. To do him posthumous justice, it was Jessop who suggested tapping the waters of the Dee to feed the Ellesmere Canal system, but it fell to Telford to design the weir, a feat he accomplished with customary panache, so much so that this purely functional arrangement has been regarded as an arcadian beauty spot ever since.

Don't stop now! Continue the last quarter of a mile to Llantysilio's little church, sign the visitor book, and offer votary thanks for the forty-four mile odyssey you've experienced from Hurleston, and all those ingredients which make the Llangollen Canal one of the great inland waterway experiences in the world.

Llangollen
Map 26

The canal could not have found a more entertaining town to terminate in. Once a year in early July, this little grey-slated Welsh town takes on a cosmopolitan atmosphere, as singers and dancers in colourful national dress take part in the famous Eisteddfod. In truth, the town is busy with tourists all summer long, as it has been since the 18th century, when early travel writers like Hazlitt and Borrow discovered the wild charm of the Vale of Llangollen. Arguably, Llangollen's heyday coincided with the residence here of the 'Ladies of Llangollen' when such august figures as Wordsworth, Sir Walter Scott and the Duke of Wellington were regular visitors. The canal wharf lies over the river from the bulk of the town, but it's just a short walk over the creaming Dee via the graceful Bishop Trevor Bridge to the centre.

Eating & Drinking

CHAIN BRIDGE HOTEL - canalside Bridge 49w. Tel: 01978 860215. Smartly refurbished hotel in idyllic setting. Bar and restaurant food for non-residents at the 'unnavigable' end of the canal. LL20 8BS

THE CORN MILL - Dee Lane. Tel: 01978 869555. Look no further than this multi-levelled modern restaurant & bar (part of the Brunning & Price group which seldom lets you down) housed within an 18th century mill whose water wheel still turns for the entertainment of diners. Balcony seating for warm days with views across the Dee to the nostalgic shufflings and shuntings of Llangollen's steam trains. LL20 8PN

GALES WINE BAR - Bridge Street. Tel: 01978 860089. Characterful wine bar offering food and also accommodation. LL20 8PF

THE GALLERY - Chapel Street. Tel: 01978 860076. Cosy family run restaurant and take-away. LL20 8NN

Llangollen (enlargement)

1 The Cornmill
2 Gales
3 Gallery
4 Ponsonby Arms
5 Samirah Spice

PONSONBY ARMS - Mill Street. Tel: 01978 447985. *Good Beer Guide* listed free house dispensing up to seven real ales. Food lunch and evening and beer garden overlooking Dee. LL20 8RY

SAMIRAH SPICE - Regent Street. Tel: 01978 861077. Indian restaurant on A5, east end of town. LL20 8HS

SUN TREVOR - adjacent Bridge 41w (Map 25). Tel: 01978 860651. Pleasant roadside pub with good (if somewhat noisy) moorings available away from the crush at Llangollen. LL20 8EG

Shopping

A surfeit of gift shops! Yet in amongst all the dross there are many genuinely attractive craft outlets. Plenty of food shops too, notably James Bailey's delicatessen (offering hugely tasty Welsh Oggies) on Castle Street where you'll also discover a butcher rejoicing in the good old Welsh name of Gwyn Davies and Chatwins the bakers who you may have encountered back in Nantwich. Watkins & Williams is a long established hardware merchants on Regent Street, as is the Blue Bay launderette.

Things to Do

TOURIST INFORMATION CENTRE - The Chapel, Castle Street. Tel: 01978 860828. LL20 8NU

LLANGOLLEN WHARF - The Wharf. Tel: 01978 860702. Base for motor-boat and horse-drawn trip boats, and also day-boat hire. Gift shop/cafe. LL20 8TA

LLANGOLLEN MUSEUM - Parade Street. Tel: 01978 862862. Local history. LL20 8PW

LLANGOLLEN RAILWAY - station riverside, below the canal wharf. Tel: 01978 860979. Daily service (April to early October, plus weekends out of season) of steam/heritage diesel hauled trains through delightful Dee Valley scenery to Corwen. Small gift shop and cafe at station overlooking the Dee. LL20 8SN

MOTOR MUSEUM - Pentrefelin Mill. Tel: 01978 860324. Absorbing collection of road vehicles. LL20 8EE

PLAS NEWYDD - Hill Street. Tel: 01978 861314. This delightful black and white timbered house set in charming gardens was the home of the 'Ladies of Llangollen', two daughters of aristocratic Irish families who lived here from 1779 to 1831. Admission charge. Open daily Easter to October. LL20 8AW *And all around are hills crying out to be climbed. A particularly fine walk leads from Bridge 45w to the 1000ft summit of Castell Dinas Bran.*

Connections

BUSES - services from Parade Street (2nd right across river bridge): 64 approx bi-hourly (not Sun) to/from Chirk via Froncysyllte; 5 every 20 mins (hourly Sun) to/from Wrexham via Trevor (for Pontcysyllte Aq.) and Ruabon railway station. Tel: 0871 200 2233.

TAXIS - Premier. Tel: 01978 861999.

BICYCLE HIRE - Safe & Sound, Chapel Street. Tel: 01978 860471. LL20 8NW *(Repairs too!)*

Montgomery Canal

Horse-boating,
Maesbury Marsh

HOWEVER popular the Montgomery Canal may become, as restoration forges ahead, its topographical hinterland will remain remote, ensuring a welcome sense of isolation. After a burst of activity generated by Frankton Locks (Map 23), the junction with the intended main line to Shrewsbury, Graham Palmer Lock and the new aqueduct over the River Perry, the canal soon loses itself in an agricultural landscape, the Berwyn and Breidden hills tantalisingly defining the western horizon.

East of the canal, Woodhouse dates from the 1770s and was designed by Robert Mylne, a Scottish architect and engineer (in the 18th century it was feasible to be both) whose curriculum vitae boasted involvement in a number of canal projects, including the Gloucester & Berkeley Ship Canal where his architectural legacy of elegantly porticoed bridge-keeper's cottages may still be appreciated. Mylne (perhaps best known for the original Blackfriars Bridge across the Thames) designed a number of bridges and country houses in Shropshire: q.v. Halston, Map 23.

In his long out of print, but still enjoyably informative Lapal Towpath Guide to the Montgomeryshire Canal, John Horsley Denton brings up the curious detour of the canal essayed circa 1799 through the Woodhouse estate at the instigation of the Rev. John Robert Lloyd, contemporary owner of the estate and a committee member of the Ellesmere Canal Company. Its use, however, was short-lived, for by 1822 the new occupant, William Owen, had the canal returned to its original route.

At Heath Houses the Shrewsbury-Chester railway crosses the canal and a derelict arm extends into the reedy precincts of what was initially a transhipment basin with the railway, but used in later years as a 'Bone Manure Manufactory'. In the mid 19th century a packet boat service operated between Newtown and Heath Houses to connect with the railway. The high-chimnied station house of Rednal & West Felton remains intact and used as a private dwelling complete with a valance-canopied timber goods shed in the grounds. In *Red For Danger*, L. T. C. Rolt described

The towpath is in reasonably good condition between Frankton Junction and Maesbury Marsh: comfortable for walkers, acceptable for cyclists. The latter, however, may find it more comfortable to divert onto the road between bridges 74 and 76.

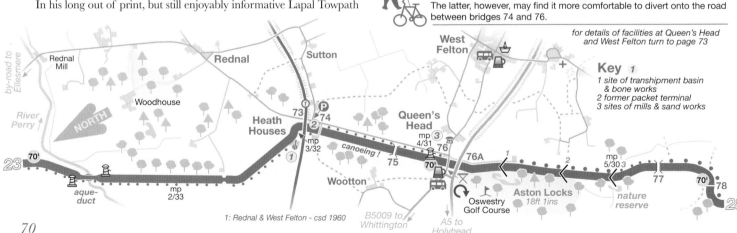

for details of facilities at Queen's Head and West Felton turn to page 73

Key 1

1 site of transhipment basin & bone works
2 former packet terminal
3 sites of mills & sand works

West Felton

Rednal Mill

by-road to Ellesmere

River Perry

NORTH

Rednal

Sutton

Woodhouse

Heath Houses

73 74

mp 3/32

canoeing !

Queen's Head

mp 4/31 3

76

75 70'

76A

1

2

mp 5/30 3

77 70' 78

nature reserve

Aston Locks 18ft 1ins

Oswestry Golf Course

Wootton

aque-duct

mp 2/33

1: Rednal & West Felton - csd 1960

B5009 to Whittington

A5 to Holyhead

23 70'

28

the fatal accident which occured at Rednal in 1865 when a double-headed excursion from Birkenhead to Shrewsbury was derailed because the driver of the leading locomotive failed to see a warning flag indicating that maintenance was underway on the track which was unable to support the heavy train.

Back on the canal, the quaint brick and timber building abutting Bridge 74 was both a warehouse and a passenger terminal for users of the packet boat. The Wolverhampton Swift Packet Boat Company advertised an astonishing schedule of just over five hours for their boat to cover the 32 miles and 22 locks involved; though, in the event, the service only lasted for a couple of years, and historians can only speculate as to whether this was because it lacked viability or its velocity was doing too much damage to the canal.

The canal parallels a busy by-road which leads to an industrial estate on the site of RAF Rednal, a Second World War aerodrome whose runways are used by go-karters and whose control tower has survived to host paintballing parties. After D-day the Americans flew wounded servicemen back to Rednal for life-saving treatment in Shropshire's military hospitals.

Skirting woodland, predominantly silver birch, the canal makes its quiet (when there are no boisterous canoeists about) way to Queen's Head, a small roadside community on Telford's road to Holyhead, the A5. In the canal's working days there was a substantial wharf here, together with a flour mill, and a sand pit linked to the canal by a narrow gauge railway which used donkeys as motive power. Travelling with his father aboard the fly-boat *Broxton*, Jack Roberts (*Shropshire Union Fly-boats* - Canal Book Shop 2015) paused briefly in 1904 to unload 'a few bags of sugar, one bag of bacon, two boxes of oranges and onions, four boxes of fruit and four boxes of kippers'. Three years earlier a boatman's nineteen year old daughter was killed at Queen's Head in an incident involving one of the wharf's cranes. Her father received £16 compensation. From 1996 to 2003 Queen's Head marked a temporary terminus in restoration terms. Aston Locks had been restored for use by boats, but controversy surrounded continuation of the canal through an area designated as being of Special Scientific Interest on account of the rare plants and insects which thrive here. The resultant truce involves responsibilities on the part of passing boaters.

Coming ...

... and Going - Frankton Locks

REVELLING in its rural isolation, the Montgomery Canal comes upon Maesbury Marsh, a quintessential country wharf with an inn, stables, boatmen's cottages and dock; the waterway equivalent of a country station before the Marples/ Beeching massacre. Business used to be brisk at Maesbury Marsh, for this was the nearest wharf to Oswestry (which, surprisingly, no one seems to have ever contemplated building a canal to) and many commodities came and went through here before the railway reached the town. Wharfinger's House, the agent's residence, bears a family likeness to Beech House back at Ellesmere. Nowadays Maesbury Marsh is the focus of much activity towards the end of the currently navigable section, as admirably exemplified by Canal Central and the horse-drawn trip-boat.

Beyond lift-bridge No.81 is the short arm which once led to Peates Mill. Sadly, the mill ceased operating in 2002 - though Lloyd's more modern animal feeds plant continues to be very much in business near Bridge 84; the company also operate mills at Wrexham, Darlington and Langport (Somerset). For their part, Peates once operated a fleet of narrowboats - not least *Cressy* of *Narrow Boat* fame - having purchased eleven craft from the Shropshire Union Company when they ceased trading in 1921. Soon, though, the development of the motor lorry made it unviable to continue carrying by canal. The grain Peates imported by way of Ellesmere Port took three or four days to reach the mill by horse-drawn boat, whereas the company's 13 ton lorry, purchased in 1932, was able to make two round trips to the port in a day. It is hardly surprising, then, that trade had all but evaporated from the canal well before the fateful breach of 1936. But in the next two or three miles you come upon the remains of some of the key industries which made it successful for a time at least. The wharf at Bridge 82 was linked by tramway to a number of collieries up on Sweeney Mountain, whilst at Crickheath Wharf another tramway connected with quarries at Llynclys and Whitehaven.

The canal's navigable status effectively ends at Gronwen Wharf, but is in the process of being restored as far as Crickheath Wharf, the next available site for a winding hole. Beyond Crickheath there is the lowered road bridge No.86 to contend with before Pant can be reached. Lift-bridge 82A is an entirely new structure, erected in the timber style favoured along the Llangollen Canal. For many years the canal south-west of Crickheath has been largely dry, its bed burgeoning with nettles, saplings and reeds.

The canal isn't the only transport mode being slowly brought back to life. Don't be surprised if you hear a steam whistle or diesel horn in the neighbourhood of Bridge 87, for a section of the old Cambrian Railways line has been re-opened from Llynclys, and the Cambrian Heritage Railways have ambitions to restore Oswestry to the railway map.

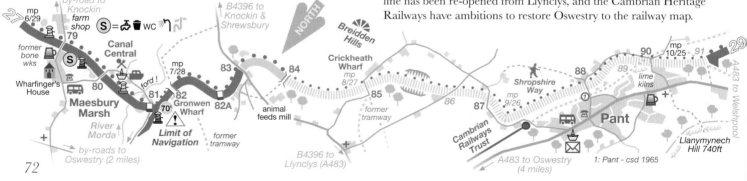

Pant was the scene of more interaction between water and rail. The standard gauge Cambrian Railways squeezed through the gap between the canal and the hillside and a station perched over the waterway by Bridge 88. Narrow gauge mineral lines came swooping down from the hillside quarries - hence the extra arch on the offside of the bridge. By Bridge 90 there is a bank of well preserved limekilns.

Queen's Head
Map 27

Eating & Drinking
QUEEN'S HEAD - canalside Bridge 76. Tel: 01691 610255. Well-appointed 'all-day' pub serving a wide choice of food and real ales. SY11 4EB

Connections
BUSES - Arriva service 70 operates half-hourly Mon-Sat and bi-hourly Sun to/from Oswestry and Shrewsbury via West Felton. Tel: 0871 200 2233.

West Felton
Map 27

Westernmost of the Ruyton XI Towns, and now spared the A5's elephantine juggernauts, the village boasts a handsome 12th century church whose most recent claim to fame is that a Miss Allegra Mostyn-Owen glided up its aisle in 1987 to be married to a Mr Johnson, Boris of that ilk. But though a bacchanalian reception ensued at Woodhouse (see main text) the marriage was dissolved in 1993.

Eating & Drinking
PUNCH BOWL - Holyhead Road. Tel: 01691 611616. Refurbished village pub. Food ex Mon. SY11 4EH

Shopping
In such remote climes you may be grateful for West Felton Stores Tel: 01691 610863 - SY11 4EA

Oswestry
(Map 27)

Birthplace of Wilfred Owen, Oswestry shares with Berwick upon Tweed the anomaly of having its football team play in a foreign country: in this case The New Saints and the Welsh Premier League. Indeed, it is a town of blurred affinities, as befits its border setting, and amply rewards detours from its adjoining canals.

Eating & Drinking
THE CURIOUS TEA ROOM - English Walls. Tel: 0750 814 8297. Charming establishment providing ideal refreshment for brief visitors. SY11 2PA

Shopping
Indoor market Wed, Fri & Sat; outdoor market Wed & Sat. Farmers Market last Friday in the month.

Things to Do
TOURIST INFORMATION & HERITAGE CENTRE - Church Terrace. Tel: 01691 662753. SY11 2TE

Maesbury Marsh
Map 28

Meresberie in the Domesday Book straddles the River Morda, a tributary of the Vyrnwy and there is evidence of Wat's Dyke a precursor of Offa's. St John's church is one of those sweet little pre-fabricated corrugated iron 'Tin Tabernacles' which travellers on the canals seem to encounter more than most.

Eating & Drinking
NAVIGATION INN - alongside Bridge 79. Tel: 01691 672958. Comfortable and well-appointed, excellent bar and restaurant food. Closed Mons, and Tue lunch. Stonehouse Oswestry-brewed ales. SY10 8JB

Shopping
CANAL CENTRAL - adjacent Bridge 80. Tel: 01691 652168. Splendid combination of village shop (specialising in locally-sourced items of viands and victuals, Welsh/Shropshire beers, quality wines etc) and coffee shop/tea room (poached eggs, bacon butties, cottage pie, soups, cakes and crumpets) housed in an eco-friendly Scandinavian style building beside the canal. Self-catering, camping and canoeing also available, as is a miniature railway. SY10 8JG

Things to Do
BYWATER CRUISES - Tel: 0794 142 9980. Utterly beguiling public and charter trips by horsedrawn boat along the Montgomery Canal. SY10 8JG

Connections
BUSES - GHA service 576 connects approx bi-hourly, Mon-Sat with Oswestry and Shrewsbury (via Ruyton XI Towns). Tel: 0871 200 2233
TAXIS - A to B. Tel: 01691 671072.

Pant
Map 28

A wayside village, more chapel than church, and well-sited to take advantage of a fully restored canal in years to come. Buzzards call over the wooded flanks of Llanymynech Hill and there are steep paths up to its nature reserve, a noted habitat of rare butterflies.

Eating & Drinking
CROSS GUNS - Rockwell Lane. Tel: 01691 830821. Main road pub open from noon daily. SY10 9QR

Shopping
Co-op stores with post office at the top of Station Road most easily reached from Bridge 88.

Things to Do
CAMBRIAN HERITAGE RAILWAYS - Llynclys. Tel: 01691 688763. Ambitious plans are on the table to re-open the railway between Gobowen and Llanymynech. At present just a short stretch is in operation (mostly at weekends during the summer months) from Llynclys (north of Pant) to Pen Y Garreg Halt. Inexpensive driver courses available. SY10 8BX

Connections
BUSES - Tanat Valley services X71 and 72 give Pant a rather better than hourly Mon-Sat link with Oswestry. Tel: 0871 200 2233.

THE canal skirts the foot of the limestone eminence of Llanymynech Hill. Probably worked for its mineral deposits as long ago as the Iron Age, it now has a golf course on its summit, notable in that fifteen of its holes are in Wales and three in England. Ian Woosnam started playing on its thymy fairways at the age of nine. Oswestry native, the novelist Barbara Pym, also golfed up there. At the point where a former railway (known as 'Rock Siding') crossed the canal (Map 28), it becomes navigable again for a short distance and a trip boat plies from Llanymynech Wharf. A high rook-roosted chimney heralds the approach to the hill's eponymous village, and the indents of old wharves eat into the offside bank. The chimney, erected in 1899 but disused within 15 years, was the flue for a Hoffman kiln used for the continuous burning of limestone. If you have ever travelled on the Settle & Carlisle railway you'll have passed a similar installation north of Settle. There is also one preserved at the Prestongrange Museum in East Lothian.

At Bridge 92 you pass into Wales; Powys since 1974, but formerly, and appropriately, the County of Montgomeryshire. The canal loses its brief navigability at Bridge 93, still intact in its hump-backed innocence, but the by-road to Tanat which crossed it has been directed across the bed of the canal, a cheese-paring act of self-indulgence by the highways authority which will come back to haunt the restorationists when they eventually re-open as far as Llanymynech. A few hundred yards to the west the canal joins a road to cross the trackbed of the old branch railway to Llanfyllin. Carreghofa, a typical GWR halt, lay on

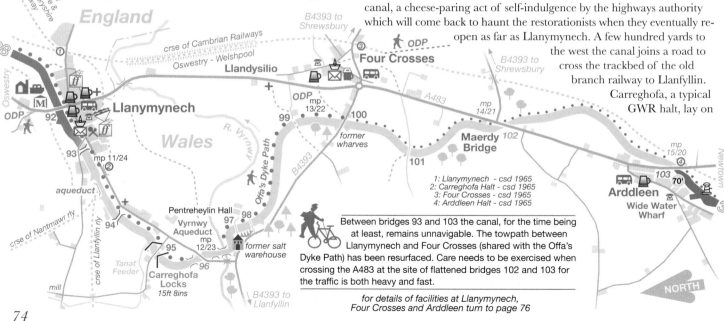

1: Llanymynech - csd 1965
2: Carreghofa Halt - csd 1965
3: Four Crosses - csd 1965
4: Arddleen Halt - csd 1965

Between bridges 93 and 103 the canal, for the time being at least, remains unnavigable. The towpath between Llanymynech and Four Crosses (shared with the Offa's Dyke Path) has been resurfaced. Care needs to be exercised when crossing the A483 at the site of flattened bridges 102 and 103 for the traffic is both heavy and fast.

for details of facilities at Llanymynech, Four Crosses and Arddleen turn to page 76

the other side of the road, deep in a cutting. When the railway was built a temporary aqueduct was constructed pending completion of the permanent one so as not to interrupt canal traffic, and its abandoned arms are still to be seen disappearing into the undergrowth. A similar phenomenon occurs at Bloxwich on the Wyrley & Essington Canal.

Disarmingly picturesque, Carreghofa Locks mark the original junction between the Llanymynech Branch of the Ellesmere Canal and the Eastern Branch of the Montgomeryshire Canal. A feeder comes in from the River Tanat and a wharfinger's office adjoins the upper lock The lock-house's modest two-storey road frontage masks a much more imposing, bay-windowed rear. It is at Carreghofa that westbound travellers enjoy their first encounter with the Montgomeryshire Canal's unique segmented paddle gear. All the more poignant, then, that notwithstanding a plaque informing them that the site was re-opened by a Baroness and the Chief Executive of the British Waterways Board in 1986, the locks remain effectively moribund.

Bridge 96 was flattened in 1980, another fiasco paying scant regard to the potential of restoration; particularly when, as John Horsley Denton sagely pointed out, its relatively low levels of traffic could have easily been diverted via Four Crosses. An embankment with flood arches leads to Vyrnwy Aqueduct, the canal's major engineering structure. Erected to the design of John Dadford in 1796, it owes more to the Brindley school of aqueduct construction than Dadford's contemporary, Telford. One of its arches collapsed soon after its opening and, in 1823, George Buck - later to build the magnificent railway viaduct at Stockport - was brought in to strengthen it. Just when he thought he had finished, the walls of the aqueduct bulged and appeared to be collapsing. Buck is said to have smote the ground in despair, but with the help of additional iron tie bars - still prominent (amidst burgeoning vegetation) to this day - the aqueduct has more or less stood its ground ever since. Cogitate upon this colourful past as you lean upon the parapet

Carreghofa Locks

Salt Warehouse

of the present and watch the waters of the Vyrnwy (which joins the Severn at Melverley, twenty miles upstream of Shrewsbury) glide below. For a more embracing view of the aqueduct, stroll down to the adjacent road bridge from 'bridge' 96.

A dog-leg bend takes the canal off the aqueduct past a handsomely refurbished salt warehouse built to last from local stone. Bridge 98, which carried the carriage road to Pentreheylin Hall, has some ornate woodwork. Arcing round the attractive hillside of Bryn Mawr, the canal reaches Four Crosses where there were separate wharves and winding holes and basins either side of Clafton Bridge (No.100). Clafton is probably a corruption of the name of a former owner of the wharf, who rejoiced in the euphonious name of Clopton Prhys. Twice in the next three miles the A483 slices across the bed of the canal, presenting a formidable obstacle to full restoration.

Llanymynech Map 29

Road traffic holds this former quarrying village hostage, bludgeoning the bucolic sensibilities of canal travellers poking their heads up the steps of Bridge 92. Walk down one side of the main street and you are in England, cross the road and you are in Wales. In common with all these border communities, the locals come over as a blurred mixture of Celt and Anglo Saxon; presumably the result of all that illicit inter-marrying down the ages. Speaking of progeny, the village's most famous native is Richard Roberts, inventor of the gasometer. Railway enthusiasts may recognise Llanymynech as the western terminus of the Shropshire & Montgomeryshire Railway, one of Colonel Stephens' impecunious outfits beloved of L.T.C. Rolt, who once propelled a platelayer's trolley from Kinnerley to Llanymynech and back in the same time scheduled for the trains; a statistic which says more about the generosity of the timetable than Rolt's athletic prowess.

Eating & Drinking

THE DOLPHIN - Tel: 01691 839672. Food and accommodation; beer garden adjacent canal. SY22 6ER
CROSS KEYS - Tel: 01691 831585. Food and accommodation. SY22 6EA
BRADFORD ARMS - Tel: 01691 830582. Food and accommodation. SY22 6EJ
GOLDEN VALLEY - Tel: 01691 830426. Chinese take-away. SY22 6EZ
BENGAL SPICES - Tel: 01691 830170. Indian restaurant and take-away. SY22 6ER
CURRY HUT - Station Road. Tel: 01691 839221. Indian take-away. SY22 6EE
There is also a cafe, and a Kebab/pizza takeaway.

Shopping

Small, though well stocked, post office stores.

Things to Do

LLANYMYNECH WHARF VISITOR CENTRE - Tel: 01691 839147. Community-run attraction with trip boat, adjoining industrial heritage area, and nature reserve. Open Sunday afternoons Easter to September. Long-term project to build a replica of the packet-boat *Duchess Countess*. SY22 6EA

Connections

BUSES - Tanat Valley service X71 links Llanymynech to Welshpool and Oswestry approximately bi-hourly Mon-Sat, whilst service 72 provides a few additional services between Llanfyllin and Oswestry. Tel: 0871 200 2233.

Four Crosses Map 29

A plaque at the far end of the whitewashed cottages by Bridge 100 recalls the boxing exploits of Dennis Powell. The long lost railway station appeared in Flanders & Swann's elegiac song *Slow Train*. Milk lorries occupy the goods yard now, whilst the old rail connected creamery has been turned into apartments.

Eating, Drinking

GOLDEN LION - Village Centre. Tel: 01691 830295. Food and accommodation. SY22 6RB

Shopping

Costcutter shop & post office at petrol station.

Connections

BUSES - Tanat Valley X71 as per Llanymynech.

Arddleen Map 29

This roadside village (whose name means 'flax-garden') marks the end of navigation north of Welshpool.

Eating, Drinking

THE HORSESHOE - Tel: 01938 590690. Food and accommodation. SY22 6PU

Connections

BUSES - Tanat Valley X71 as per Llanymynech.

Pool Quay Map 30

Severnside settlement of considerable antiquity. Mid-nineteenth century maps depict a barytes grinding mill, corn mill, sawmill, flannel factory, blacksmiths and malt house with drying kilns. Now solely the relentless traffic on the A483 destroys the inherent calm of this lost inland port.

Eating & Drinking

THE POWIS ARMS - Tel: 01938 590255. Former coaching inn with inglenook, real ale, home cooked food and accommodation. Open from 11am. The sign authentically depicts a SUCCCo flyboat in juxtaposition with segmental paddle gear. SY21 9JS
Refreshments are occasionally available in St John's church.

Holiday Lets

CROWTHER HALL LOCK COTTAGE - Tel: 01938 590543. Self-catering accommodation. Quarry-tiled floors, wood-burning stove and exposed beams but no phone or television - sounds heavenly! SY21 9JU

Guilsfield Map 30

A substantial village famous for its church and its football team, and how often can you say that! The church is dedicated to St Aelhaiarn, a 7th century Welshman. Pevsner was enthusiastic enough to label it 'one of the richest medieval church interiors in the county'. Guilsfield FC play in the Huws Gray Alliance against such stalwart opponents as Holyhead Hotspur, Prestatyn Town and Mold Alexandra.

Eating & Drinking

KING'S HEAD - Tel: 01938 555930. SY21 9NJ
OAK INN - Tel: 01938 559246. SY21 9NH

Shopping

Spar post office stores on Arddleen Road.

Connections

BUSES - Tanat Valley X71 as per Llanymynech.

A DOZEN enchanting miles to play with, and nobody comes! How has it come to pass that the restored Welshpool section of the canal, stretching from Arddleen (Map 29) to Berriew (Map 32) is, with the honourable exception of the Heulwen Trust trip boats, virtually unused? It remains outside the province of a mere guide book to provide a political answer, but to the casual, if heartfelt observer, the effort put into restoring this part of the Montgomery Canal in the 'eighties and 'nineties appears tantamount to a Sisyphean waste of belief and resources. If the canal is ever to be successfully linked to the main network, a good proportion of this section will effectively have to be 'restored' all over again.

Burgedin Locks were re-opened in the summer of 1998. Above the locks the Guilsfield Arm joins the main canal. An amble along the B4392 offers glimpses of its course and the

occasional overbridge remaining intact. Without the unstinting belief of its support groups, the main line might have become equally derelict.

Burgedin Locks drop the canal by sixteen and a half feet to the sump level of the canal, making the Montgomery a peculiarity in a world where most man-made navigations climb up to, and descend from, a central summit. At Wern there is a slipway, winding hole and picnic area; the latter on the site of a former corn mill which derived its power from the sump level's plentiful supply of excess water produced by boats using the locks in either direction. Southwards from Wern the canal rides along an embankment above marshy ground, a remnant of the swamp which surrounded the Severn before it was drained early in the 19th century. On the far side of the river stand the Breidden Hills,

continued on page 78:

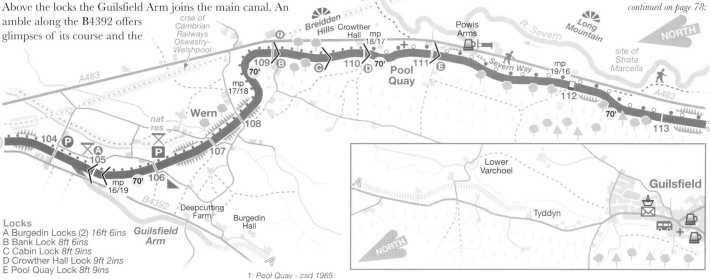

Locks
A Burgedin Locks (2) *16ft 6ins*
B Bank Lock *8ft 6ins*
C Cabin Lock *8ft 9ins*
D Crowther Hall Lock *9ft 2ins*
E Pool Quay Lock *8ft 9ins*

1: Pool Quay - csd 1965

continued from page 77:

seldom out of sight since you left Frankton. Now you can enjoy them in detail: quarry-scarred Breidden Hill itself, the most northerly summit, topped by a monument to Admiral Rodney by way of thanks for using Mont-gomeryshire timber in the building of his navy; and Moel y Golfa to the south with a memorial to Ernest Burton, King of Romanys. In a curious echo of the 18th Century naval memorial, the locality played host to a clandestine radio station built during the Second World War to enable the Admiralty to keep track of its vessels. Dominated by a trio of Eiffel Tower-shaped, seven hundred foot high masts (originally earmarked for erection in Ceylon!), the site continued to be strategically significant throughout the Cold War and into the 21st Century as a means of communicating with Britain's nuclear submarine fleet. The station closed and the masts were demolished in 2003.

Bank Lock is the first (or last) of four in close proximity which raise (or lower) the canal by some 35 feet. Each chamber has its segmented ground paddles, though these are not in general use. Crowther Hall Lock is the deepest on the canal. The charming lock cottage is available for holiday lets. A bench commemorates a 'land girl' who worked at Crowther Hall farm and lived in the lockside cottage in the late 1940s. Pool Quay's delightful Victorian church, with its elaborate and distinctively carved timber belfry, overlooks the next pound.

Pool Quay marked the head of navigation on the River Severn. It was, as the name suggests, the port, or quay, for Poole, an earlier name for Welshpool; though previously the settlement, the site of a notable Cistercian monastery, was known as Strata Marcella. The monks brought industry to the banks of the Severn and harnessed the river's power to drive a flour mill, textile works and forge. The Severn could only be navigated this far upstream in winter when there was sufficient depth of water, and with the advent of canal and railway transportation, carrying on the river had ceased by the mid 19th century. The railway, part of the Cambrian system absorbed by the Great Western, closed in 1965, being part of the same route from Whitchurch to Welshpool whose scars are encountered at various points along the Llangollen Canal. One of the station masters at Pool Quay was

a bee-keeper who won prizes for his honey.

South of Pool Quay, Long Mountain assumes the vertical mantle of the Breiddens. Deep in its trench - unless sufficient rain has fallen on the hills of mid-Wales to make it break its banks - the Severn snakes about its valley floor, a modest watercourse difficult to associate with the broad navigable river of Gloucestershire featured in our *Severn & Avon Companion*. Briefly eluding the A483, the canal hides under the protective, wooded, sheep-grazed skirts of Yr Allt - an altogether delightful stretch of waterway.

Crowther Hall Lock

The towpath south of Pool Quay is well used, as it forms both part of the Offa's Dyke Path (Chepstow-Prestatyn) and the Severn Way (Plynlimon-Bristol Channel), but north of Pool Quay it is unsurfaced and can become somewhat overgrown in summer; hardly impassable, but watch out for nettles and brambles if you're wearing shorts.

31 MONTGOMERY CANAL Welshpool 4mls/3lks/3hrs

ROAD schemes seldom benefit canals. You only have to look as far as the Montgomery's flattened bridges to see the truth of this. Yet, paradoxically, the Welshpool by-pass twice came to the rescue of the town's canal: initially in 1969 when it was proposed to route the new road along the bed of the long moribund waterway, the threat of its loss crystallising a latent enthusiasm for the canal; then again in 1992/3 when the by-pass was finally constructed along a different course, allowing the previously flattened Gallows Tree Bank Bridge (117) to be rebuilt with headroom for boats. Final completion of the by-pass and subsequent rebuilding of Whitehouse Bridge (120) in 1998 resulted in the release of those dozen or so miles of navigable waterway. Initially everything looked rosy. A pair of Anglo Welsh hire boats were outstationed at Welshpool, a day boat was made available for hire and a number of privately owned craft were drawn to the route. But such initiatives proved unsustainable, and a vicious circle of under-use and weed growth has - Heulwen Trust trip boats apart - rendered the canal effectively disused once more, a tragic state of affairs which does little to promote the benefits of canal restoration to the wider public gaze.

Milepost 21 commemorates the fly boat captain Jack Roberts. Buttington Wharf (just north of Bridge 115) was an early development under the Montgomery Canal restoration programme, being home to *Heulwen Sunshine*, a specially built trip boat for the disabled which pioneered navigation on this length of canal from 1976. The wharf, popular with local people, has picnic tables and a trio of preserved limekilns; discipline being

continued on page 80:

for details of facilities at Welshpool turn to page 81

continued from page 79:

maintained by a rotundly sculptured wharfinger and his dog. The Heulwen Trust's trip boats, however - now offering public trips to boot - are based at the more recently constructed Gungrog Wharf by Bridge 116.

A Leisure Centre overlooks Bridge 117. Two notable industrial premises lined the canal on its way into Welshpool: on the towpath side a gasworks flourished briefly before being resited when the railway opened; on the offside a large mill, grandiosely known as the Welshpool Company for the Manufacture of Flannel by Steam, stood canalside until the 1930s, latterly being employed as an ordnance works and, briefly, for the manufacture of motorcycles. Some flannel workers terraced cottages remain occupied.

Bungalows with neat gardens and Victorian villas - one with a monkey puzzle tree and a gazebo - herald the approach to the town centre. Empty mooring pontoons emphasise the dearth of boats. Bridge 118A once carried the celebrated Welshpool & Llanfair Light Railway across the canal to its transhipment sidings by the standard gauge Cambrian Railways station, now it carries shoppers to Tesco. Eight miles of the 2ft 6ins gauge line pass through delightful countryside from Welshpool's Raven Square station to the rural terminus of Llanfair Caereinion.

Immediately south of the old railway bridge a small aqueduct, dated 1836, carries the canal over Lledan Brook. The semi-circular weir was part of a scheme whereby water was extracted by a local mill. Welshpool's canalscape is quite delightful, the heart being centred on the old canal yard with its imposing and photogenic warehouse which now serves as a local museum. Interestingly, archive photographs reveal that the overflow from Town Lock provided power for the water wheel of an adjoining

Welshpool Trip Boat

corn mill. Beyond the lock, the canal effects its exit from Welshpool rapidly, the urban environs being exchanged for sports grounds, housing and, before long, the gracious landscape of Powis Castle's parkland. A right angled turn takes the canal under Bridge 120 and along a short new section of the canal, wide and deep compared to the original course which is still in water and well utilised for fishing. The extensive premises bordering the canal on the far side of the A490 belonged to the sawmill and smithy of the Powis Estate. Excess water from the canal was used to power the yard's machinery until the canal became disused and silted up, thereafter the yard's machinery was converted to electric power in the 1940s. The yard's two-storey, stone-built office and blacksmith's shop remains clearly visible from the towpath. Stephen Hughes' *The Archaeology of the Montgomeryshire Canal*, though long out of print, contains fascinating detail of the sawmill, and indeed many of the other buildings and installations associated with the canal.

Hugging the western slopes of the broad Severn valley, the canal affords commanding views of the wooded flanks of Long Mountain to the east. The high spired church is at Leighton, whose towered hall - partly designed by Pugin - is also visible to the south. Belan Locks soon follow, raising the level of the canal by a total of twelve feet. Close by the lock cottage, with its neatly kept garden, is a group of amazingly ornate black and white cottages, occupied in bygone days by agricultural workers. On the horizon the green hills of Mid Wales enticingly beckon the southbound traveller onwards. But pause for a moment, turn and enjoy again the most splendid view of the Breidden Hills. Sometimes, it seems, the landscape - like life itself - is even better when looking back.

Welshpool
Map 31

If ever a town deserved to be linked to the canal network, Welshpool is it. One can only look at the empty moorings and weep. Monday is the day to immerse yourself in the town when, as well as the general market, the weekly sheep and cattle market makes its colourful presence felt, even though the cattle market itself has moved away from its previous canalside location to the vicinity of Buttington Wharf. Down from the hills, farming folk congregate in the town to buy and sell, and to assuage the loneliness of their isolated lives in the freemasonry of the auction ring. And all day the town's pubs hum to the sing-song accents of Mid Wales, whilst the steeply climbing High Street, relatively quiet on other days, reverberates to the passage of cattle lorries, Landrovers and battered old cars plastered in the mud and slurry of far-flung farms.

Eating & Drinking
ANDREWS - High Street. Tel: 01938 552635. Award-winning fish & chips. SY21 7JP
THE CORN STORE - Church Street. Tel: 01938 554614. Restaurant. SY21 7DL
HOWARD'S RESTAURANT - Coed-y-Dinas. Tel: 01938 555545. Breakfasts, lunches, teas and regular themed evening meals at the garden, home and country centre to the south of the town. SY21 8RP
OLD STATION RESTAURANT - Old Station. Tel: 01938 556622. SY21 7AY
ROYAL OAK HOTEL - Severn Street. Tel: 01938 552217. Imposing hotel offering bar and restaurant food for non-residents. Local Welsh beers such as Monty's and Stonehouse usually on tap. SY21 7DG
THE SMITHFIELD BELL - Mill Lane. Tel: 01938 559472. New-build Marston's pub and restaurant adjacent Bridge 118. SY21 7BL

Welshpool & Llanfair Railway

Shopping
Good facilities for a relatively small town reflect Welshpool's importance as a centre for a wide agricultural hinterland. Tesco, Morrisons and Sainsbury's all have supermarkets in the town, but there are plenty of local retailers too, such as Rikki Lloyd's butchers on High Street who've won prizes for their steak and kidney pies. There's a useful launderette adjacent to the imposing Victorian Town Hall on High Street and Brooks bicycle shop on Severn Street near the canal wharf. There are food markets on Mondays and Saturdays centred on the Town Hall and Broad Street.

Things to Do
TOURIST INFORMATION CENTRE - Vicarage Garden Car Park (adjoining Bridge 118A). Tel: 01938 552043. Heulwen trip-boat bookings. SY21 7DD
POWYSLAND MUSEUM - Canal Wharf. Tel: 01938 554656. Charming displays of local history in the restored canal warehouse. SY21 7AQ
THE OLD STATION - Severn Road. Tel: 01938 556622. Conglomerate of specialist outlets housed in handsome former station building. SY21 7AY
COED-Y-DINAS - Tel: 01938 555545. Attractively laid out garden centre and country store. Impressive food hall. Farmers Market on 1st Friday in the month. Cafe/restaurant. SY21 8RP
POWIS CASTLE, MUSEUM & GARDEN - Tel: 01938 551929. Famous garden, medieval castle and Clive Museum displaying treasures from India including textiles, armour, bronzes, jade, ivory etc. National Trust shop and licensed tea room. SY21 8RF
WELSHPOOL & LLANFAIR RAILWAY - Tel: 01938 810441. One of the 'Great Little Trains of Wales'. Services operate March to October, though not necessarily daily in the quieter months either side of high summer. Departures from Raven Square station at western edge of town. SY21 7LT

Connections
BUSES - Tanat Valley service X71 links Welshpool approximately bi-hourly (Mon-Sat) with Oswestry via Arddleen, Four Crosses, Llanymynech and Pant shadowing the course of the Guilsfield Arm in the process. At Welshpool this connects with Celtic Travel service X75 which runs at similar intervals to Newtown via Berriew, Garthmyl and Abermule. Tel: 0871 200 2233.
TRAINS - Arriva Trains Wales services to/from Shrewsbury, Newtown and the Cambrian Coast. Tel: 03457 484950.

NOT so much a canal, more a Welsh hymn tune, the Montgomery shadows the Severn's broad flood plain. Your head is turned, and it is difficult to avoid subjectively labelling it the network's prettiest waterway. All the more damning, then, that this supposedly fully restored section is so utterly devoid of boats. Indeed, so unused has it become that, irony heaped on irony, rampant vegetation renders it practically unnavigable. So shrug your shoulders and let the scenery work its balm. Callow Hill, at 1,247 feet, dominates the skyline to the east, part of the wonderful Shropshire hill country in the vicinity of Bishop's Castle. Brithdir Lock occupies a most delightful setting, its by-pass weir forming a pond-like feature beside a well-kept lawn. Swans abound - real and realised - whilst a copse of oak, ash and copper beech trees, set on an almost perfectly-rounded hill, provides an exquisite backdrop.

Beyond Berriew Lock, the canal is carried on an embankment across the Rhiw Valley and on to Berriew Aqueduct. An 1889 rebuild in brick of an earlier stone structure, the four-arched aqueduct (two river and two land arches) takes the waterway over the fast flowing waters of the Rhiw and the minor road into Berriew. The village's football team, who ply their trade in the Mid Wales League along with other Montgomery Canal associates such as Four Crosses and Welshpool, have a surprisingly impressive 'stadium'

between the canal and the river.

Flattened Bridge 129, carrying the B4385 road to Berriew, brings to an end the supposedly navigable section from Arddleen. The winding hole is filled with water lilies. Financial constraints meant that construction of the Montgomeryshire Canal stalled in 1797 and for over twenty years Garthmyl, just over 16 miles from Carreghofa, was its terminus. What came to be known as the Western Branch through to Newtown was not completed until 1821. At Garthmyl was concentrated a series of wharves, warehouses, maltings, coal yards, stables and limekilns, and in its heyday the village must have been the scene of intense activity. It still is, but only from cars and lorries thundering along the A483, the widening of which in 1949 obliterated most of the wharf area, although the old maltings are still in evidence beside an infilled section of canal. Garthmyl is also notable in that it is the closest point on the canal to Montgomery - just three miles away along the B4385.

Map labels: Moat Farm; Wernllwyd; mp 24/11; Severn Way; mp 25/10; 122; 123; 124; Horseshoes; Brithdir Lock 9ft 1ins; 125; 70'; 126; Luggy Aqueduct; Luggy Brook; Callow Hill 1247ft; A483; 81; mp 26/9; Berriew Lock 8ft 5ins; 127; 128; black-smith; 70'; Berriew; B4390 to New Mills; NORTH; old fort; Berriew Aqueduct; Mus of Sculpture; Cwmgwydd; 70' 129 nursery; mp 27/8; River Rhiw; River Severn; Glansevern Hall; Montgomery War Memorial; 130; 131; 132; Garthmyl; by-road to Bettws Cedewain; 31

Berriew
Map 32

Enchanting village beside the River Rhiw, with clusters of black and white cottages huddling around the church of St Beuno's and a handsome 18th century single span stone bridge downstream of some falls.

Eating & Drinking
THE HORSESHOES - on A483 by Bridge 125. Tel: 01686 640282. Comfortably refurbished country pub open from noon daily. SY21 8AW
LION HOTEL - village centre. Tel: 01686 640452. Half-timbered inn offering accommodation, restaurant and bar meals. SY21 8PQ
THE TALBOT HOTEL - Tel: 01686 640881. Comfortable small hotel idyllically located beside the River Rhiw. Bar and restaurant food. SY21 8PJ
LYCHGATE COTTAGE - village centre. Tel: 01686 640750. Tea room and deli. Closed Suns. SY21 8PG
UPPER RECTORY - Tel: 01686 640930. Restaurant offering seven course tasting menus Thur-Sat evenings from 7pm, reservations essential. Plus accommodation in one bedroom self-catering cottage, and Shepherd's Hut. SY21 8AN

Shopping
Post office stores open daily 7am-7pm (8am Sat & Sun), butcher and small gift shop.

Things to Do
ANDREW LOGAN MUSEUM OF SCULPTURE - beside the river. Tel: 01686 640689. A 'glittering, sparkling, fantasy wonderland' founded by the originator of the Alternative Miss World contest. Shop selling jewellery and sculpture. Mostly only open summer weekends. Cafe and shop. SY21 8AH
GLANSEVERN HALL - Tel: 01686 640644. 25 acres of garden in grounds of Greek Revival house on banks of the Severn. Open Spring-Autumn Tue-Sat and Bank Hol Mons 10.30am-5pm. Tea room. SY21 8AH

Brithdir

Navvy and cyclist

Bridge 140

Connections
BUSES - Celtic Travel service X75 operates approximately bi-hourly services Mon-Sat to/from Newtown and Welshpool. Tel: 0871 200 2233.

Garthmyl
Map 32

Wayside village on A483 Chester-Llandovery main road.

Eating & Drinking
NAGS HEAD - adjacent bridge 131. Tel: 01686 640600. Gastro-pub with boutique accommodation. SY15 6RS

Accommodation
PENLLWYN LODGES - Brynllwyn Lane. Tel: 01686 640269. Self-catering timber lodges in woodland overlooking the canal. Adjoining golf course and restaurant. SY15 6RU

Connections
BUSES - as Berriew.

Abermule
Map 33

Expanding village at the confluence of the Mule and Severn. A lovely cast iron bridge spans the Severn adjacent to canal Bridge 147. Large characters carry the inscription: 'THIS SECOND IRON BRIDGE CONSTRUCTED IN THE COUNTY OF MONTGOMERYSHIRE IN THE YEAR 1852'.

Eating & Drinking
THE ABERMULE - village centre. Tel: 01686 630117. Village pub with restaurant open from 4pm Tue-Fri and from noon Sat & Sun. SY15 6ND

Shopping
Village stores.

Things to Do
KINGFISHER KAYAK - Glanhafren Hall (Bridge 143). Tel: 0747 456 2669. Kayak and canoe hire. SY15 6NA

Connections
BUSES - Celtic Travel X75 and Tanat Valley 71.

33 MONTGOMERY CANAL Abermule 4mls/2lks

CANOEING is encouraged along this otherwise unnavigable stretch of the Montgomery Canal and portaging points are thoughtfully provided either side of fixed or flattened bridges. 'The towpath, in default of one along the Severn, is the pleasantest and easiest walk along the valley' wrote Brian Waters, the poet and topographical writer in *Severn Stream* published in 1949, and half a century has happily done nothing to make one argue with his view; indeed, the towpath has become officially adopted as the route of the Severn Way between Pool Quay and Newtown and National Cycle Route 81between Welshpool and its latter terminus.

Two more flattened bridges (coincidentally in the same year as Brian Waters' book was published) provide a stark reminder of the difficulties facing the return of full navigable status. William Pugh, one of the prime movers in the canal's extension westwards, was born at Pennant. Wealthy, educated, and philanthropic, he built the Flannel Exchange in Newtown and put so much money into the canal and the local economy that he was forced to flee across the Channel to escape his creditors, dying a pauper's exile in 1842.The creditors may have been confounded, but retrospectively we can thank Pugh for this ravishingly beautiful canal.

By Bridge 140 there's a most life-like wooden sculpture of a navvy. At Brynderwen Lock the towpath briefly changes sides to accommodate a former coal wharf. On the road side of the adjoining corrugated iron clad warehouse an authentic sign still proclaims SHROPSHIRE UNION RAILWAYS & CANAL CO. GENERAL CARRIERS. Grants have been awarded in recent years to sustain the intrinsic biodiversity of the Montgomery Canal, especially in relation to its rare and indigenous floating water plantain *Luronium natans*.

Abermule is remembered for being the site of a railway accident in 1921. Two trains - an Aberystwyth-Manchester express and a Whitchurch-Aberystwyth stopping train - collided head on along a stretch of single track; 17 people were killed and 36 injured. A happier railway memory is of the branchline from Abermule which threaded the gorge of the River Mule to the famous sheep-rearing centre of Kerry. Closed in 1956, in its final days cattle trains struggled up the grass-grown line solely to serve monthly sheep fairs.

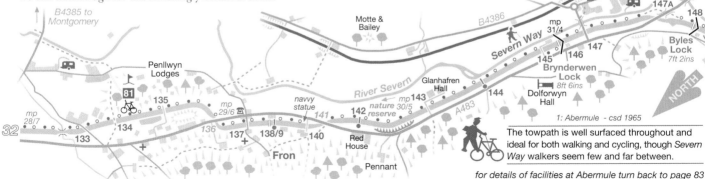

1: Abermule - csd 1965

The towpath is well surfaced throughout and ideal for both walking and cycling, though *Severn Way* walkers seem few and far between.

for details of facilities at Abermule turn back to page 83

SAVOURING its proximity to the Severn, the Western Branch of the Montgomeryshire Canal probes deeper and deeper into the delectable, sheep-rearing heart of mid-Wales, 'The Mont', as it is bluntly but affectionately known to its core supporters, reaches its illogical conclusion on the outskirts of Newtown. Illogical, that is, because even the most zealous revivalist of the canal's fortunes would conclude that restoration of the Montgomery's last couple of miles, together with its once extensive terminal basin, is too far-fetched a proposal to bear close scrutiny.

Newhouse Lock is the last of a restored trio which would suggest to the random passer-by that the canal is more fully navigable than is the case. Bechan Brook is crossed on a three arched aqueduct before Bridge 152 carries the B4389 road into the hamlet of Aberbechan, the last settlement of any sort before Newtown. Freestone Lock is derelict and gateless, its keeper's house roofless, windowless and strangled by trees, whilst the canal bed beyond is a mass of rushes. Pwll Penarth Nature Reserve is accessible

from the towpath. The Severn broadens and Penarth Weir becomes audible, seeming to mock the moribund canal's inactivity. The weir was constructed by the canal's engineers in 1819 to convey water from the river into the canal. A cast iron sign again reminds us that this was once the property of the Shropshire Union Railways & Canal Company.

Barely discernible, Dolfor Lock stands alongside a large sewage works. The Shropshire Union Canal Society have relaid the hedge here; full restoration may be a pipe dream but small contributions like this are still worthwhile. The canal as such vanishes, but its course may be followed along a well defined pathway.

Apart from an abrupt rise in the asphalt path, there is no obvious clue as to the site of Rock Lock, the most westerly on the canal. Quarter of a mile further on, an old pumping house which drew water for the canal up from the River Severn restores your faith that there was indeed a waterway here once. Together with an adjoining cottage and a cast iron overbridge, it looks more like a former railway station. Briefly the course

continued on page 86:

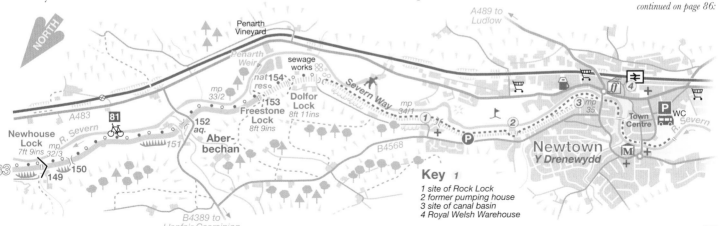

Key 1
1 site of Rock Lock
2 former pumping house
3 site of canal basin
4 Royal Welsh Warehouse

continued from page 86:

of the canal runs at the rear of terraced houses, but beyond this point the canal has been built over and it is necessary to follow the riverside Severn Way into the centre of Newtown.

Should this abrupt end appear an anti-climax after the thirty-five mile journey from Welsh Frankton, consider instead the heady days of the nineteenth century when the area was a cornucopia of limekilns, foundries, coal and timber wharves. No less than seven dock arms extended from the main basin, each capable of holding two narrowboats simultaneously. By the twentieth century Newtown's mills were mainly mechanised and, whilst some used water power, others were steam operated and received their coal by canal. The last to do so were the Commercial Mills of Jones, Evans & Co, manufacturers of blankets, shawls and knitted goods. When they closed in 1935, they were still using 20 tons of coal a week. Mined in the collieries at Chirk, it was delivered by Tom Moody in his narrowboat *Endeavour*. Bearing in mind the ever deteriorating state of the Montgomery Canal, the round trip from Chirk probably took around a week to complete and it is doubtful whether he was able to carry any other traffic. When Jones, Evans & Co closed in 1935, Tom Moody stopped work, leaving George Beck as the last surviving boatman on the canal, until the breach of the following year put him out of business too.

Newtown   Map 34

The second town (Llanidloes is the first) that the Severn encounters on its long hike south to the Bristol Channel. Moreover, charm oozes from almost every non-porous brick in this market town whose longevity belies the mundanity of its name. Edward I granted the town a charter in 1279 but it was not until the nineteenth century that Newtown grew significantly with development of the woollen industry - at its zenith it acquired the sobriquet 'The Leeds of Wales'. Newtown's most famous son was Robert Owen (1771-1858), the successful capitalist whose socialist ideals inspired the Co-operative movement. His statue stands in Shortbridge Street and his tomb in the grounds of St Mary's ruined riverside church. Prominent on the southern edge of the town by the railway station is the Royal Welsh Warehouse. Erected by Pryce Pryce-Jones, a local draper, it is thought to have been the first mail order business in the world, numbering amongst its customers, Florence Nightingale and Queen Victoria. Pryce-Jones patented the Euklisia Rug, a forerunner of the sleeping bag and is credited with the concept of the parcel post. Another fine feature of this most likeable town is the plethora of impressive nonconformist chapels: Zion Baptist, Welsh and English Calvinistic, Wesleyan et al. On Severn Street a plaque commemorates local novelist Geraint Goodwin (1903-41) whose life and literary output was cut short by tuberculosis.

Accommodation

YESTERDAYS - Severn Street. Tel: 01686 622644. Superior guest house accommodation for the benefit of tired walkers. Huge Welsh breakfasts. SY16 2AG

Eating & Drinking

JARMAN'S FISH RESTAURANT - High Street. Tel: 01686 625505. Filling fish suppers for hungry walkers. SY16 2NX

MIRRENS - Parker's Lane. Tel: 01686 621120. Stylish restaurant and tapas bar open daily for lunch and dinner (lunch only Sun). SY16 2LT

SPORTSMAN - Severn Street. Tel: 01686 623978. *Good Beer Guide* listed town centre pub owned by Monty's Brewery from Montgomery. SY16 2BQ

Shopping

Chain stores lurk in the Bear Lanes Precinct and Ladywell Shopping Centre. Pearsonites are more discerning and make for the charming indoor market (Tue, Thur, Fri and Sat) or the launderette on Severn Street should all this walking have resulted in embarrassing dishevelment.

Things to Do

CLEAN ENERGY CENTRE - Gas Street. Tel: 0772 272 2863. Electric bike hire. SY16 4LE

ROBERT OWEN MUSEUM - The Cross, Broad Street. Tel: 01686 626345. Museum (housed in glorious Arts & Crafts 'confection' of a building) telling the remarkable story of the man who inspired the Co-operative movement. Admission free. Open Mon-Sat throughout the year. SY16 2BB

W. H. SMITH MUSEUM - High Street. Tel: 01686 626280. The shop has been restored to its original state when first opened in 1927 and on the first floor is a small museum open shop hours. SY16 2NP

TEXTILE MUSEUM - Commercial Street (north bank of Severn). Taken over by support group from cash-starved council. Enquire locally as to opening times.

Connections

BUSES - Celtic Travel X75 (Mon-Sat) parallels the Montgomery Canal offering opportunities for one-way walks between Newtown and the likes of Abermule, Garthmyl and Berriew. Tel: 0871 200 2233.

TRAINS - Arriva Trains Wales services to/from Welshpool, Shrewsbury and the Mid-Wales coast. Tel: 03457 484950.

TAXIS - Station Cabs. Tel: 01686 621818.

Monmouthshire & Brecon Canal

Bridge 105, Gilwern

87

PERCEIVED by many canallers as being too remote and short to be worthy of exploration, what is now known as the Monmouthshire & Brecon Canal was built as two separate waterways, the Monmouthshire Canal and the Brecon & Abergavenny Canal. The former, opened in 1799, ran for eleven miles from the Usk Estuary at Newport to Pontnewynydd, north-west of Pontypool, with an eleven mile branch from Malpas to Crumlin. The latter, opened throughout in 1812, linked Brecon with Pontymoile, junction with the Monmouthshire, a distance of some 33 miles. In 1865 the Brecon & Abergavenny Canal was bought by the Monmouthshire Company.

Commercial trade ended in the 1930s and the Monmouthshire Canal was largely abandoned, but the Brecon & Abergavenny Canal survived, primarily as a water feeder. With financial support from local authorities, the waterway was reopened for navigation between Brecon and Pontymoile in 1970. Subsequent restoration work has seen the limit of navigation pushed south as far as Five Locks, Cwmbran. Further proposals exist to restore the Mon & Brec all the way down to Newport and thus provide a link with the rest of the inland

Pontymoile Basin

A472 to Crumlin

Tesco

Town Centre

Pontypool

Dry Ski Slope

51 A

52

Junction Cottage

WC

Griffithstown

50A

hosp.

50

51

52

53

Five Locks

60'

Cwmbran Tunnel

Sebastopol

46

60'

49

cemy

Forge Hammer

47 48

49

492

Open Hearth

Pontypool & New Inn

Pontnewydd

Cwmbran

Afon Llwyd

A4051

A4042 to Newport

New Inn

Abergavenny

NORTH

Key
1 site of Panteg Steel Works
2 site of Pontypool Road mpd 86G
3 site of Phoenix Galvanising Works
4: site of Lower Mills Sheet Works

Closed Railway Stations
1: Upper Pontnewydd - csd 1962
2: Pontnewydd - csd 1958
3: Pontrhydyrun Halt - csd 1962
4: Sebastopol - csd 1962
5: Panteg & Griffithstown - csd 1962
6: Pontypool Blaendare Road - csd 1962
7: Pontypool Clarence Street - csd 1964
8: Pontypool Crane Street - csd 1962

1 Low Headroom

Scale: 2½ inches to a mile

waterway network (somewhat challengingly) by way of the Usk and Severn estuaries. But for the time being navigability begins, or ends, at Five Locks, where a lowered road bridge and a flight of derelict locks bar any further progress south. A mooring basin and winding point have been provided and the surroundings are bland but unthreateningly suburban.

The first half mile or so of navigable canal is in the care of Torfaen County Borough Council as opposed to the Canal & River Trust. Often pea soup green with algae, the canal water betrays a prevalent hesitancy amongst boaters to venture south of Pontymoile. But an absence of boats is more than compensated for by high numbers of pedestrians - both purposeful and lolling - and cyclists (ditto!) on the metalled towpath.

Cwmbran Tunnel - just 87 yards long with a path over the top - looks rather disconcertingly like a toy, albeit one cradled endearingly in a leafy bower. Such bucolic overtones are shortlived. At Bridge 47 TCBC hand over responsibility to CRT and urbanisation sets in. Some may find the post-industrial communities of Pontnewydd, Sebastopol (which gained its name from the Crimean War) and Griffithstown (named after Henry, the first stationmaster at Pontypool Road) too dour for their holiday-making sensibilities, but this is the *real* South Wales, a throwback zone of terraced houses, telegraph poles and ice cream van jingles.

Just by the congenial Open Hearth pub a surviving Monmouthshire Canal milepost informs that the Newport terminus of the canal lay eight miles to the south. New housing occupies the site of Panteg Steel Works, closed in 2004. The rather forbidding hospital bordering the offside of the canal between bridges 50 and 51, was originally the Pontypool Poor Law Institution. The concrete abutments of a bridge which carried a narrow gauge railway into the infirmary can be seen beyond Bridge 50. Converted into a cycleway, the trackbed of the Newport & Blaenavon Railway crosses the canal on high, skewed girders by Bridge 51.

Pontymoile Basin marks the former junction of the Monmouthshire and Brecon & Abergavenny canals. Not without irony the busy dual-carriageway A472 running west to Crumlin and Ebbw Vale was built over the course of an abandoned railway, itself built over the course of the Monmouthshire Canal. History can be awfully unkind to transport undertakings. Nowadays Pontymoile Basin is a popular leisure asset for nearby Pontypool. A tea bar and picnic site draw the locals. Here, in the canal's working past, boats were assessed for tolls as they went from one canal to the other. Close by, an aqueduct - the tallest on the Mon & Brec - carries the canal over the Afon Llwyd ('Grey River') where the young turks of the neighbourhood are apt to dive noisily in on hot days.

Cwmbran   Map 35
A 'new town', though established as long ago as 1949, best known nowadays for the economically vital production of Jammie Dodgers and Wagon Wheels.
Eating & Drinking
OPEN HEARTH - Wern Road, Sebastopol (between bridges 48 & 49). Tel: 01495 763752. The lost tradition of steel-making gives this friendly canalside pub (and *Good Beer Guide* fixture) its curious name. Real ales and a wide-ranging menu make this probably the best port of call in the vicinity. NP4 5DR
PAGES FISH BAR - Bridge 48. Tel: 01495 753185. Reputedly one of the best in South Wales! NP4 5BQ

Connections
TRAINS - Arriva Trains Wales offer links with the outside world and the possibility of one-way towpath walks to/from Abergavenny. Tel: 03457 484950.
TAXIS - Gwent Cars. Tel: 01633 866665.

Pontypool   Map 35
A much older town than Cwmbran, having grown dramatically during the industrial revolution. The jewel in its tarnished crown is a large municipal park.
Eating & Drinking
Tea bar at Pontymoile Basin open Wed-Sun 10.30am-4pm. Harvester Restaurant (Tel: 01495 751551) KFC and McDonald's at nearby junction of A472/A4042.

Shopping
Petrol station shop 5 mins from Pontymoile Basin. Tesco supermarket and town shops 20 mins away.
Things to Do
PONTYPOOL MUSEUM - Park Road. Tel: 01495 752036. Splendid museum of local history housed in Georgian stable block. Open Tue-Fri 10am-5pm, Sat & Sun 2-5pm. Shop and refreshments. NP4 6JH
Connections
TRAINS - Arriva Trains Wales services to/from Cwmbran and Abergavenny etc. from station best reached on foot via Bridge 53. Tel: 03457 484950.
TAXIS - Gwent Cars. Tel: 01495 751010.

FORMING the eastern boundary of the Brecon Beacons National Park - not that the landscape beyond appears any less meritorious - the canal winds picturesquely between frequent overbridges. The vast works down below Bridge 59 was erected by British Nylon Spinners in 1948 and was one of the largest employers in the district for the best part of half a century, later being absorbed by ICI and subsequently DuPont. Now it hosts myriad activities, many of them local and regional government based. In 1971 it gained a neighbour in the shape of a pharmaceutical works erected for the Parke Davis company. It was said to have the longest internal corridor in the UK. Subsequently it fell out of use and was used for filming episodes of *Dr Who* in 2007. Now much of it has been demolished and the site is to be redeveloped.

A local landmark is the Folly Tower, erected in the 1770s as a summer house and lookout for deer hunting. During the Second World War it was more or less completely demolished against fears that enemy aircraft might employ it to pinpoint the munitions plant at Glascoed. Not until 1995 was it fully rebuilt.

Throughout its working existence, the canal's main traffic was in coal. Other significant cargoes included iron and timber. Barges were typically of nine foot beam and just over sixty feet in length. They were horse-drawn and could carry twenty tons. The last recorded toll - for a boatload of lime - was recorded at Llangynidr (Map 42) in 1933.

Eating & Drinking

HORSE & JOCKEY - Usk Road (east of Bridge 55). Tel: 01495 762721. Pretty thatched and whitewashed pub with emphasis on food. From noon. NP4 0JB

STAR INN - Old Abergavenny Road (Bridge 62). Tel: 01495 785319. Country pub and dining from 11am daily. NP4 0JF

HORSESHOE INN - Old Abergavenny Road. Tel: 01873 880542. Well appointed and welcoming country pub open lunch & evenings Mon-Thur and from noon throughout Fri-Sun. NP4 8QZ

GOYTRE ARMS - Penperlleni (10 mins walk east of bridges 71/72). Tel: 01873 880376. NP4 0AH. *The village also boasts a fish & chips bar.*

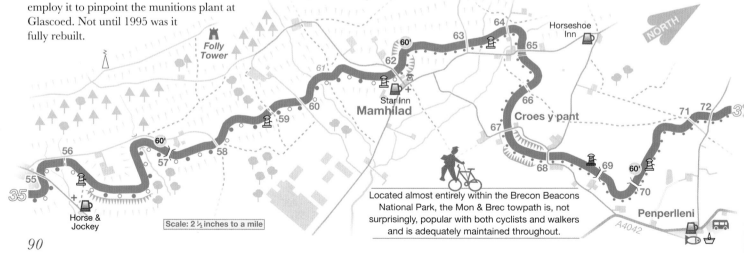

Located almost entirely within the Brecon Beacons National Park, the Mon & Brec towpath is, not surprisingly, popular with both cyclists and walkers and is adequately maintained throughout.

Scale: 2½ inches to a mile

TREE-LINED, secretive, and often demarcating the boundaries of traditional hill farms, the canal sustains its idyllic progress between, to the west, the steep flanks of a ridge which separates it from the once heavily industrialised South Wales Valleys and, to the east, a pastoral landscape levelling out past clumps of woodland towards the banks of the Usk. Frequent occupation bridges - most humped, some flat-decked - punctuate the canal's progress along the 367 foot contour line. Thomas Dadford Junior's feat of essaying a twenty-five mile pound in such mountainous surrounds is a remarkable achievement. Occasionally you find yourself wishing, uncharacteristically, that there were less trees, because they do tend to mask the views, though, by the time the bridge numbers are in the early eighties, you begin to glimpse the mountains which lie ahead, notably Sugar Loaf to the left and the Ysgyryds (Skirrids), Fach (Small) and Fawr (Great), to the right.

Goytre Wharf has long been a showcase for the Mon & Brec, and continues to fulfill that role, having recently been acquired outright by the ABC Leisure Group

from the Canal & River Trust. A microcosm of a typical canal wharf of its era, it attracts a surprising number of visitors by road; though if they are curious to see the canal in its historic setting, or simply desperate for a cup of tea and a slice or two of cake is anyone's guess. Certainly the setting, with its aqueduct and rank of lime kilns, is worth savouring, although visitor moorings - squeezed between angler's perches and a water point - are at a premium.

Between bridges 77 and 78 there is a circular cattle drinking pond fed from the canal. The house on the offside by Bridge 81 features an internal boathouse. Glimpsed below through the trees, Llanover House belonged to one Benjamin Hall, who, as Commissioner of Works, gave his name to London's most famous horological landmark, Big Ben. To cross precipitous water courses, the canal is twice forced into horseshoe curves: challenging engineering feats in their day, whilst demanding of vigilant maintenance even now; but hugely scenic in effect.

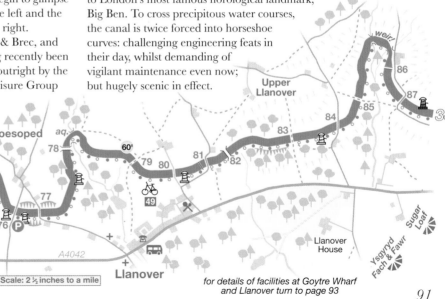

1: ABC/Red Line

Scale: 2½ inches to a mile

for details of facilities at Goytre Wharf and Llanover turn to page 93

91

38 MONMOUTHSHIRE & BRECON Abergavenny 3mls/0lks/1½hrs

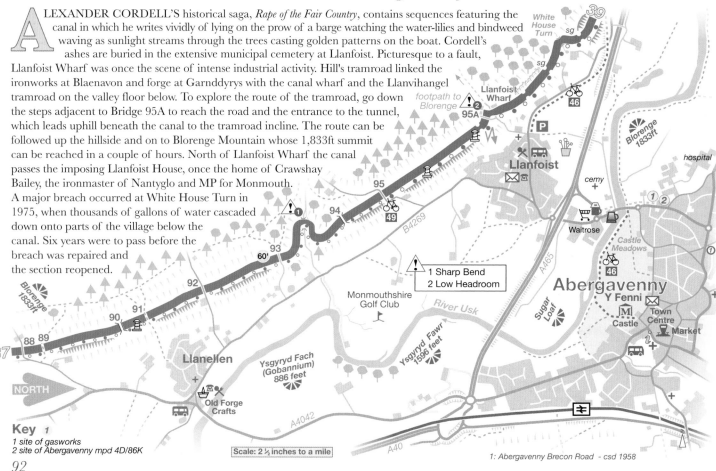

ALEXANDER CORDELL'S historical saga, *Rape of the Fair Country*, contains sequences featuring the canal in which he writes vividly of lying on the prow of a barge watching the water-lilies and bindweed waving as sunlight streams through the trees casting golden patterns on the boat. Cordell's ashes are buried in the extensive municipal cemetery at Llanfoist. Picturesque to a fault, Llanfoist Wharf was once the scene of intense industrial activity. Hill's tramroad linked the ironworks at Blaenavon and forge at Garnddyrys with the canal wharf and the Llanvihangel tramroad on the valley floor below. To explore the route of the tramroad, go down the steps adjacent to Bridge 95A to reach the road and the entrance to the tunnel, which leads uphill beneath the canal to the tramroad incline. The route can be followed up the hillside and on to Blorenge Mountain whose 1,833ft summit can be reached in a couple of hours. North of Llanfoist Wharf the canal passes the imposing Llanfoist House, once the home of Crawshay Bailey, the ironmaster of Nantyglo and MP for Monmouth. A major breach occurred at White House Turn in 1975, when thousands of gallons of water cascaded down onto parts of the village below the canal. Six years were to pass before the breach was repaired and the section reopened.

> ⚠ 1 Sharp Bend
> 2 Low Headroom

Key 1
1 site of gasworks
2 site of Abergavenny mpd 4D/86K

Scale: 2½ inches to a mile

1: Abergavenny Brecon Road - csd 1958

Goytre Wharf
Map 37

The Waterfront Cafe (Tel: 01873 880899 - NP7 9EW) provides refreshments, and ABC offer self-catering for up to four in Aqueduct Cottage - Tel: 0330 333 0590.

Llanover
Map 37

Comfortably furnished, Hummingbird coffee shop (Tel: 01873 881044) is a pleasant walk down from Bridge 80. They do a nice line in local gifts too. NP7 9HA

Llanellen
Map 38

Village tucked below the canal on the busy Pontypool to Abergavenny main road. Small convenience store and Old Forge Crafts (Tel: 01873 854811 - NP7 9HT) which offers gifts and *Welsh* teas. Bus service X33.

Llanfoist
Map 38

The remains of the ironmaster Crawshay Bailey lie in the cemetery of the pretty little church of St Faith's (a 3rd Century martyr) which you pass on your steep descent from the canal. Note the B&ACCo initials!

Eating & Drinking
BRIDGE INN - Merthyr Road. Tel: 01873 854831. *Good Beer Guide* listed inn overlooking the Usk. Open from 11am (noon Sun). Food and accommodation. NP7 9LH
SPICE LOUNGE - Merthyr Road. Tel: 01873 855720. Indian restaurant & t/a daily from 5.30pm. NP7 9LP

Self-Catering
Beacon Park Cottages have two idyllically situated properties sleeping six and two respectively for holiday hire at Llanfoist Wharf - Tel:01873 858277.

Abergavenny
Map 38

Canallers may legitimately wish that Hamelin of Ballon had sited his 11th Century castle on the *west* bank of the Usk and that Abergavenny had subsequently developed much closer to where the canal was eventually dug. Similarly, railway enthusiasts may mourn the closure of the Heads of the Valleys line in 1958, prior to which they could have caught a local train at Govilon and passed triumphantly over the Usk into Abergavenny (Brecon Road) in a cloud of smoke and steam. More mundanely, nowadays you will need to catch a bus or call a taxi, or make the mile long journey under your own steam. But make it one must, for it is well-nigh impossible to resist the siren call of the town hall tower - positively Ruritanian in its lofty eminence - and the town itself, however one eventually reaches it - is of enormous appeal.

Eating & Drinking
ANGEL HOTEL - Cross Street. Tel: 01873 857121. *Good Beer Guide* listed coaching inn offering bar and restaurant food and accommodation. NP7 5EW
GRECO - Cross Street. Tel: 01873 854840. Ultra retro cafe for high carb hits. NP7 5ER
GURKHA CORNER - Nevill Street. Tel: 01873 855800. Nepali cuisine. Sister est. in Brecon. NP7 5AD
KINGS ARMS - Nevill Street. Tel: 01873 855074. Comfortable accommodation and 'gastropub' food. We enjoyed coracle-caught sewin! NP7 5AA
MARKET STREET FISH & CHIPS - Market Street. Tel: 01873 855791. Restaurant/take-away. NP7 5SD
NICHOLLS - Frogmore Street. Tel: 01873 853306. Department store coffee shop with outdoor courtyard open daily 9am-4.45pm. NP7 5AH
PREZZO - Frogmore Street. Tel: 01873 857390. Italian cooking from a usually reliable chain. NP7 5AW
WALNUT TREE INN - Llanddewi Skirrid. Tel: 01873 852797. Michelin starred dining at internationally famous restaurant 3 miles NE of A. NP7 8AW

Shopping
There's a Waitrose supermarket less than 20 minutes walk from Bridge 95A, but it is Abergavenny's independent shops - like Rawlings the butchers on Market Street, Edwards butchers and delicatessen on Flannel Street, and Marches Delicatessen on Nevill Street - that really contribute to the pleasure of shopping here. Look out too for Nicholls department store on Frogmore Street, Abergavenny Music on Cross Street and Broadleaf Books secondhand bookshop on Monk Street. The lively retail market which they're so proud of takes place on Tuesdays in and around the handsome market hall. There are additional retail markets on Fridays and Saturdays, a vibrant Flea Market on Wednesdays and a Farmers Market on the fourth Thursday in the month. By the way, don't miss Burton's men's clothes shop retaining its 'Tailor of Taste' slogan and gold-leafed list of towns with branches. Abergavenny's growing reputation as a food centre culminates each September in an increasingly influential event which has been labelled 'the Glastonbury of food festivals'.

Things to Do
TOURIST INFORMATION - Monk Street, Monmouth Road. Tel: 01873 853254. NP7 5HL
ABERGAVENNY MUSEUM AND CASTLE - Castle Street. Tel: 01873 854282. Open daily March-October, closed Sundays November-February. Displays trace the history of the town from Roman times. NP7 5EE
ST MARY'S PRIORY - Monk Street. Tel: 01873 858787. Imposing priory church described as 'the Westminster Abbey of South Wales'. Adjoining 13th century tithe barn houses the Abergavenny Tapestry which took sixty ladies four years to stitch. Locally sourced refreshments and souvenir shop. NP7 5ND

Connections
BUSES - Cardiff service (X4) calls at Llanfoist, Govilon and Gilwern; Brecon buses (X43/43) stop at Crickhowell; X3/X33 runs to/from Cardiff via Llanover, Pontypool & Cwmbran. Tel: 0871 200 2233.
TRAINS - Arriva Trains Wales services to/from Shrewsbury and Cwmbran etc. Tel: 03457 484950.
TAXIS - Station Cars. Tel: 01873 857233.

GOVILON AND GILWERN provide alliterative punctuation to your journey as the canal veers north-westwards out of Abergavenny's orbit, and in doing so introduces a not entirely unwelcome atmosphere of urbanisation: all those arboreal glades can become a tad repetitive when dawdling along at one and a half miles an hour. Govilon Wharf hosts the Canal & River Trust's maintenance yard as well as Govilon Boat Club. The wharf was once an interchange point with tramroad, and later railway, traffic. In *The Forgotten Railways of South Wales* (David & Charles, 1979) James Page considered the Merthyr Tredegar & Abergavenny Railway the most spectacular in South Wales. The trackbed is now a well-surfaced footpath and cycleway worth exploring, perhaps as part of a circular itinerary incorporating the towpath. Adjacent Bridge 97B stands Llanwenarth Baptist Church whose fellowship, dating from 1652, is reputedly the oldest in Wales. With its hipped roof and cream

painted facade, it presents a memorable sight from the canal, backed by the summit of Sugar Loaf. As is common in Wales, the churchyard - entered through a fine wrought iron gateway - contains many handsome tombs and headstones.

Much encumbered, William Bliss alighted at Govilon station to begin his canoeing trip along the Mon & Brec Canal vividly described in *Rapid Rivers*, published in 1935. He wrote of this section of the canal: 'The canal made a bend to cross the little Llanwenarth brook, and between that and Gilwern there were wonderful open views from the canal itself up the Usk Valley. I was glad I had come. It was late May, and everything was green and happy and there was no-one there but me'. There are still wonderful views up the Usk Valley and across to Sugar Loaf and the Black Mountains, and everything is still 'green and happy'. As for there being 'no-one there', well we can't promise that, but by virtue of its isolation, the Mon & Brec is *Bliss*fully quieter than the main canal network. Govilon's

Blorenge

Gilwern Hill

Llanelly

Llanwenarth House

B

99 100 101 102 103 104 105 106 107

60' 60' 60' 60' 60' 60'

97 98 96

Govilon

A465

Sugar Loaf 1955ft

Monmouthshire

Gilwern
(see enlargement)

A4077

R. Clydach

River Usk

Powys

Pen Cerrig calch 2302ft

1: Govilon - csd 1958
2: Gilwern Halt - csd 1958

Scale: 2½ inches to a mile

S = ♿ 🚮 🚰 🏕 WC

1 Low Headroom
2 Blind Bend
3 *Very* Low Headroom

parish church nestles snugly beneath the canal's embankment. It dates from the middle of the 19th Century, before which villagers crossed the Usk by ferry to pay their devotions. The lych-gate commemorates a former village schoolmaster who rejoiced in the unforgettable name of Ivor Tossell. It was at Llanwenarth House, south of Bridge 100, that Mrs Cecil F. Alexander, an Irish poetess, composed the words for the hymn *All Things Bright and Beautiful* in 1848. Certainly she had a plethora of 'purple headed mountain(s)' to inspire her muse.

At Gilwern a right-angled bend takes the canal dramatically across the Clydach Gorge on a ninety foot high embankment. On the south side was the Clydach Iron Company's wharf and a connecting tramroad, branches of which led to further wharves and to the Clydach Basin, now the base of Castle Narrowboats who, probably uniquely in the UK, offer electric powered boats for hire charged from points along the canal. Visitor moorings encourage exploration in the neighbourhood of the aqueduct where steps lead down into the bosky gorge.

It was in the neighbourhood of Bridge 106 that a breach occurred in October 2007 which resulted in the canal being closed for over a year. Subsequently, sixteen miles of canal were closed for a geotechnical survey to be carried out and ninety leaks were discovered. A hundred thousand fish had to be relocated. In the end some £15 million was spent on refurbishing the canal, an outlay commensurate with the canal's annual contribution to the local economy. From Bridge 106 a rocky path climbs to the tiny village of Llanelly whose parish church, dedicated to St Elli, contains stained glass windows depicting the coal and iron industries; frustratingly, the church tends only to be open at weekends.

Govilon Map 39
Interpretive Boards usher you entertainingly around a number of Heritage Trails. The War Memorial is notable in that it lists a female civilian, one May Prosser, believed to have been killed in a munitions factory.
Eating & Drinking
TAFARN Y BONT - Church Lane (best approached via the aqueduct steps). Tel: 01873 830720. Open lunch & evening Mon-Thur and from noon 'til 'closing time' Fri-Sun. Village pub with good choice of food. NP7 9RP
Shopping
Convenience store open 7.30am (8am Sun) to 9pm.
Connections
BUSES - Stagecoach X4 operates hourly Mon-Sat between Abergavenny and Cardiff (an interesting journey through 'The Valleys') and proceeds bi-hourly in an easterly direction to Hereford. Stagecoach service 3 provides additional local links. Tel: 0871 200 2233.

Gilwern Map 39
The industry of the Clydach Gorge has withered with age and been replaced by commuter properties handy for the Heads of the Valleys highway. But there remain fascinating nooks and crannies to uncover, whilst this is a useful point for feeding & watering, especially if you're not planning to visit the fleshpots of Y Fenni.

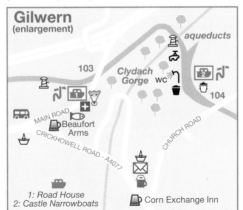

Gilwern (enlargement)
aqueducts
103
Clydach Gorge wc
104
MAIN ROAD
Beaufort Arms
CRICKHOWELL ROAD - A4077
CHURCH ROAD
Corn Exchange Inn
1: Road House
2: Castle Narrowboats

Eating & Drinking
BEAUFORT ARMS - Main Road. Tel: 01873 832235. Bar and restaurant food, open daily from 11.30am. Accommodation. NP7 0AR
CORN EXCHANGE INN - Crickhowell Road. Tel: 01873 832404. Open from 4pm Mon-Fri and noon Sat & Sun. Beers from Brains and Wye Valley. NP7 0DG
VILLAGE FISH BAR - Main Road. Tel: 01873 832040. Open Wed-Sat, noon to 8pm. Award-winning fish & chips cooked fresh to order, so you may like to telephone ahead rather than queue. NP7 0AS
Shopping
A good butcher (Bromfields - Tel: 01873 268686), pharmacy, and charming little gift shop (Road House Narrowboats - Tel: 01873 830240 - who also offer B&B) on Main Road leading down from Bridge 103. Convenience store (open from 7am daily) and post office in petrol station on A4077; plus second convenience store at foot of Main Road.
Connections
BUSES - as Govilon.

EXCHANGING Monmouthshire for Powys (or, more properly in the Pearson scheme of things, Brecknockshire) the canal glides enchantingly beneath the quarried flank of Llangattock Mountain and above the broad valley of the Usk. You don't get anywhere fast on this shallow canal, yet nor should you want to; this is Stevenson's 'travelling hopefully', not your daily commute.

Northbound through Bridge 110 you catch your first glimpse of Table Mountain squatting amiably over the little town of Crickhowell, a community approaching perfection. Try mooring for the night near Bridge 111, then, as daylight fades, watch the lights twinkling in the cottages and farms far across the valley, like a sea of stars in a cloudless sky.

It was on this section, close by Bridge 110, that cutting of the canal began in April 1796. Visitor Moorings just south of Bridge 116 provide the easiest access to Crickhowell, which lies about three-quarters of a mile away across the Usk. Walk down through the churchyard on a path which comes out at Crickhowell Bridge which from downstream appears to have thirteen arches, whilst from upstream twelve, and this before you've patronised the bar of the Bridge Inn.

Bridge 118 is known as Workhouse Bridge, but the object of this haunting association has thankfully been transformed into a boutique bed & breakfast establishment. Concrete edged, the canal north of Bridge 119 appears to solicit mooring but appearances, in this case, are extremely deceptive, for the sides are extremely shallow.

Mynydd Llangattock
1735ft

Beacon Park

Llangattock
Wharf
115
114
Llangattock
Boat Club
60'

113

112

110

111

Heron's Rest
Marina
60'

108
109

39

Llangattock

116

117

Ffawyddog

118
119
120

industrial
estate

Old
Rectory

P

Powys

A4077

B4558
Dardy

River Usk

Castle

A40

Crickhowell

Table Mountain
1481ft

Town
Centre

Pen Allt-mawr
2360ft

NORTH

Pen Cerrig-calch
2302ft

(S) = ♨ ♿ 🗑 ⚓ WC

Llangattock   Map 40

Llangattock takes its name from the imposing church of St Catwg, founded in the 6th century and rebuilt in the 12th. Tucked away down a narrow lane, the village stocks and whipping post are contained within its grounds.

Eating & Drinking

OLD RECTORY HOTEL - Access from Bridge 116. Tel: 01873 810373. Country house hotel with 9 hole golf course offering breakfast, lunch, tea and dinner to non-residents. NP8 1PH

Connections

BUSES - service 43 connects Llangattock with Crickhowell (and thence Abergavenny), and with Brecon (via Llangattock and Talybont) five times a day, Mon-Sat. Tel: 0871 200 2233.

Crickhowell   Map 40

This peach of a little town hit the headlines in 2015 when local businesses moved 'offshore' to publicise the tax loopholes flaunted by multi-nationals. Normally, however, life here is lived much less antagonistically. Indeed, they were cooling off in the Usk on one occasion when we visited, though given the quixotic nature of the local climate, we can't guarantee you'll be greeted by similar scenes of abandonment. What we can safely promise, however, is that Crickhowell - increasingly well known for its annual Walking Festival at the beginning of March - will rub off on you as favourably as it always does us. The name is the Anglicised form of Crug Hywel, the rampart and the ditch stronghold of Hywel Dda - now known as Table Mountain, which overlooks the town. The ruined castle dates back to Norman times.

Eating & Drinking

BEAR HOTEL - High Street. Tel: 01873 810408. Immensely comfortable and welcoming 15th century

Table Mountain

coaching inn; all beams, big fireplaces and flagstones. Bar and restaurant meals plus very tempting accommodation. *Good Beer Guide* listed. NP8 1BW
BRIDGE END INN - Tel: 01873 810338. The nearest pub to the canal, open from noon daily for bar and restaurant food, plus accommodation. Delightful beer garden perched above the Usk. NP8 1AR
COURTROOM CAFE - Market Hall. Tel: 01873 812497. Refreshments in historic setting. NP8 1BD
DRAGON INN - High Street. Tel: 01873 810362. Stylish hotel & restaurant rivalling The Bear. NP8 1BE

LATTE DA - Beaufort Street. Tel: 0789 075 1755. Beguiling shabby chic tea room offering breakfasts, lunches and teas and open from 9am to 5pm daily. Try the American pancakes, replete with bacon and the fluffiest scrambled eggs you'll ever taste. NP8 1AD
YUMMY KITCHEN - Standard Street. Tel: 01873 811177. Traditional fish & chips, pizzeria and chargrill take-away. Open Mon-Sat 10am-9pm. NP8 1BP

Shopping

Supermarket-free Crickhowell is a heavenly place to saunter around and shopping here is the pleasure it ought to be, the emphasis being on characterful individual retail outlets such as Askews Bakery, Grenfell's Grocery, Cashells and Richards butchers shops, and Webbs Department Store (est 1936). Nicholls, (est 1925) another department store also has branches in Abergavenny and Brecon. Tower Gallery on High Street is home to Usk Valley Artists' Co-operative. Across the street is a tiny, yet award-winning independent bookshop called Book-ish. Also on High Street is Black Mountain Gold, an artisan chocolate maker. Bacchus (Beaufort Street) stocks a good choice of wine together with a thirst-inducing range of Welsh beers. There is a Lloyds bank, and the post office is at the southern end of the town on Beaufort Street. Small market on Thursdays.

Things to Do

CRiC - Beaufort Street. Tel: 01873 811970. Exemplary modern information centre with cafe, upper storey gallery and internet facilities. Open daily from 10am until 5pm (1.30pm Sun). NP8 1BN

Connections

BUSES - services X43/43 connect Crickhowell approximately bi-hourly, Mon-Sat, with Brecon (via Llangattock and Talybont 43) and Abergavenny. Tel: 0871 200 2233.

TAXIS - Crickhowell Taxis. Tel: 01873 811764.

Pontymoile

Sebastopo[l]

Griffithstown

Llanfois[t]

M&B MISCELLANY 1

ARE there any limits to the beauty of the Mon & Brec, you catch yourself wondering rhetorically, and, given the visual evidence at your disposal, you are in no position to demur. Why, even those of an industrial archaeological bent, used to salivating their way around the murkier and more arcane corners of the BCN can enjoy a Pavlovian response in the limekilns and tramroads which continue to evoke recollections of this canal's industrial origins.

Amongst other events, Glanusk Park hosts the annual Green Man music festival. The estate was established in 1826 by Sir Joseph Bailey who, like his brother Crawshay (Map 38), had made his fortune in iron production. The original mansion was demolished after being set on fire by the Army, who had requisitioned it during the Second World War, but the imposing Dower House remains. In 1876 the estate's gamekeeper was shot dead whilst trying to apprehend poachers. The stone 'barn' by Bridge 125 formerly saw use as a stable for boat horses.

Backed by the conifer forested slopes of Myarth Hill, and the craggy outcrops of Darren and Bryniog, stands Gliffaes. It is an Italianate country house, erected towards the end of the 19th century for a Rev. W. West, a well-travelled clergyman who had managed to mislay three of his family's fortunes in the process. Since the nineteen

thirties it has been used as an hotel and is notable for its twin campaniles. When the vicar finally ran out of money the house passed to a man called Sir Shirley Salt, the son - and this will appeal to users of *Pearson's Canal Companion to the Leeds & Liverpool Canal* - of Titus Salt of Saltaire, Bradford. Sir Shirley had married one of the Baileys of Glanusk and had, not surprisingly, become enamoured of the neighbourhood as much as one of its female residents. Gliffaes translates sweetly as 'dewy field' and, by all accounts, the hotel offers considerable luxury to its guests, though unfortunately there is no way to reach it easily from the canal without getting wet.

Approaching Llangynidr (difficult for mere Anglo Saxons to pronounce, but try 'Clan-gun-idder') an aqueduct carries the canal over Nant Cleisfer, and the beauty simply continues ...

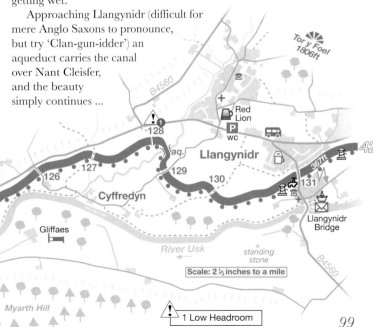

TWENTY-FIVE idyllic miles of northbound lock-free cruising come abruptly to an end at Bridge 132. It makes, however, a pleasant change for boaters to have something to do and non-boaters to have something to watch whilst, like English wickets going down in a Test Match, you don't just get one or two locks, but five in relatively quick succession. Designed - like most locks in South Wales - to accommodate boats of 63ft length and 9ft beam, they are spread over less than a mile and lift the canal up by 48 feet. Local practice is to leave the locks empty with bottom gates open; something of an inconvenience as it means you always have to fill the lock first when locking down, or empty it afterwards when locking up. The apparently random numbers (64-68) date from the Great Western Railway's acquisition of the canal in 1880. Further evidence of GWR ownership includes boundary posts and the lozenge-shaped weight-limit signs familiar to those who know the Stratford-on-Avon Canal.

Between the first and second locks the canal crosses the River Crawnon on a sizeable aqueduct equipped with a plug and conventional windlass to drain this section of the canal. Public moorings are provided nearby, presenting the opportunity to be lulled to sleep by the babbling waters of the Crawnon. Hirers from Country Craft - one of six bases on this isolated canal - can avail themselves of offside moorings handy for a delightful path which runs alongside a feeder into the woods.

Canal & River Trust volunteers are often in attendance to help you through Lock 65; thus 'Llangynidr Welcome Station' invariably lives up to its name. Attended by woodland, the top three locks are overlooked by the almost perfectly rounded summit of Tor y Foel. A former workhouse - subsequently two agricultural workers' cottages - stands beside Bridge 136. Today it serves as a highly desirable private residence.

A stroll downhill from Bridge 138 stands the little Tudor church of St Tetti at Llanddetty. Steeped in history, one of its most remarkable associations

Map labels:

Usk Valley Walk
Tor y Foel 1806ft
Beacons Way
NORTH
Llangynidr Locks (5) 48ft 0ins
68 67 66 65
415ft
Glawcoed
134
133
64
132
41
136
135
137
138
139
139A
140
141
Llanddetty Hall
Llanddetty
+
Buckland Old Mill
Llangynidr
feeder
aqueduct
65
134
Country Craft
S
Coach & Horses
133
Scale: 2½ inches to a mile
S = WC
Buckland Hall
suspension bridge
B4558
Mynydd Llangorse 1661ft
Ashford House
Alt yr Esgair
Ashford Tunnel ! 1 375 yards
! 1 Very Low Headroom
crse of Brinore Tramroad
crse of Brecon & Merthyr Railway
Talybont
aq.
143 144
Star
White Hart
Caerfanell
8
43
lime kilns
143
142
60'
144
145
The Travellers
Usk Inn
Talybont on Usk
Afon Caerfanell

Route March, Llangynidr

dates back to the Civil War when a Parliamentarian parishioner by the name of Jenkin Jones appropriated the incumbency, using the church as a farm. He was apparently milking his ewes when he heard of the landing of Charles II at Dover in 1660. Instantly he mounted his horse, rode through the churchyard, discharged a pistol and cried out: 'Ah, thy old whore of Babylon, thou'll have it all thy own way now' before riding off and never being seen in the neighbourhood again. A bullet hole in the priest's door corroborates the story to this day. Nearby a decrepit suspension bridge spans the Usk. It was probably erected to enable people from Buckland Hall to visit the church. Buckland was requisitioned by the War Office in 1939 and became a military hospital, receiving many soldiers wounded at Dunkirk. In excess of three hundred servicemen are laid to rest in St Tetti's churchyard.

Llanddetty Hall offers bed & breakfast, but can trace its origins back to the 17th century, having been originally built by the aforementioned Jenkin Jones. Down the centuries it has been occupied by many interesting people, not least the promoter of the Brinore Tramroad and a widow who was to become the wife of a certain Benjamin Disraeli.

Ashford Tunnel - so low in the middle that you can get a crick in your neck negotiating it - has no towpath; in bygone days horses went over the top and boats were poled through. It was built as a 'dig and fill tunnel', whereby a cutting was first made and the tunnel built, then the earth was put back over the tunnel. At the southern portal a plaque commemorates the fact that, after a period of closure for repair, the tunnel was officially reopened on 5th May 1985, the ceremony being performed by Mr Trevor Luckcuck; his name is depicted in large capital letters. Mr Luckcuck was, as many of you will know, British Waterways' Deputy Chief Executive at the time. None can gainsay the immortality of petty officialdom! Beyond the tunnel the B4558 runs in close proximity to the canal, the traffic appearing unnervingly rapid. A reedy winding-hole adjacent to Bridge 142 recalls the existence of a transhipment wharf between the canal and the Brinore Tramroad which was opened in 1815 to link the canal with a colliery near Rhymney. An interpretive board and replica wagon elucidate. A hefty pipe conveys the Newport water main across the canal.

Like someone coughing at a hushed moment in a classical concert, Talybont briefly interrupts the Mon & Brec's default setting soundtrack of plashing water, mewing buzzards and bleating sheep. Just this once you're prepared to forgive the intrusion, though, because you've been *dying* for an ice cream since Gilwern. A skeletal girder bridge acts as a sort of lych-gate to the village. This once bore the mountainous Brecon & Merthyr Railway across the canal at the commencement of a severe 1 in 38 gradient known as the 'Seven Mile Bank'. Regrettably the line lost its passenger services in 1962, resulting in the closure of such outlandishly named and unnervingly isolated stations as Torpantau, Pontsticill and Pentir Rhiw. Chunks of it to the south-west of Talybont have been appropriated by the 55 mile Taff Trail which links Brecon with Cardiff. Parts of it have been relaid as the narrow gauge Brecon Mountain Railway.

Just after the awkwardly-sited Bridge 143, an aqueduct carries the canal across the Afon Caerfanell which flows down off the Brecon Beacons through the massive Talybont Reservoir to join the Usk nearby. An embankment carries the canal parallel to the village's main street. The Visitor Moorings here fill up early. On the offside a cottage bears the inscription 'B&ACCo. 1843'. Lift bridge 144 is electrified and cannot be raised at certain times in the morning and afternoons during school terms lest its use might delay the neighbourhood's darling children from their lessons, or more importantly, their tea.

Llangynidr · Map 41

Set in perhaps the most dramatic section of the Usk Valley, Llangynidr is undoubtedly one of the shiniest jewels in the Mon & Brec crown. The village comprises three distinct parts: Upper Llangynidr, half a mile from Bridge 129; Cwm Crawnon close to the 'Coach & Horses'; and Lower Llangynidr, also known as Coed-yr-ynys, which is down by the Usk. The latter is the most pleasing, an enchanting jumble of cottages by the ancient and extremely narrow bridge over the Usk.

Eating & Drinking

COACH & HORSES - Cwm Crawnon Road (adjacent Bridge 133, Map 42). Tel: 01874 730245. Self-branded 'canal boat pit stop'. NP8 1LS

RED LION HOTEL - Duffryn Road, Upper Llangynidr. Tel: 01874 730223. *Good Beer Guide* listed 15th century coaching inn. Bed & Breakfast. NP8 1NT

Shopping

WALNUT TREE STORES - Lower Llandgynidr (Bridge 131 is closest on canal). Tel: 01874 730309. Post office stores 8am to 8pm (7pm winter weekends). NP8 1NA

Connections

BUSES - service 43 runs five times a day, Mon-Sat, to/from Abergavenny (via Crickhowell) and Brecon (via Talybont). Tel: 0871 200 2233.

Talybont-on-Usk · Map 42

This wayside village, where the 'Taff Trail' joins/leaves the canal, is a launch pad for all manner of outdoor pursuits. Of rather shorter duration is 'Vaughan Walk', a two and a half mile waymarked trail celebrating the haunts of the 17th century poet, Henry Vaughan, who lies buried in St Bride's churchyard just across the Usk.

Eating & Drinking

CANAL SIDE CAFE - Tel: 01874 676663. Popular cafe adjoining village stores. Open daily 9am-5pm throughout the summer months, shuts 3pm in winter. Evening meals Friday and Saturday nights April to September. Take-away food as well. LD3 7YJ

STAR INN - canalside by aqueduct. Tel: 01874 676635. *Good Beer Guide* entry. B & B. LD3 7YX

THE TRAVELLERS - adjacent Bridge 142 (Map 42). Tel: 01874 676233. Restaurant & rooms. LD3 7YP

USK INN - Station Road. Tel: 01874 676251. LD3 7JE

WHITE HART - adjacent Bridge 143. Tel: 01874 676227. Traditional pub grub and bunkhouse accommodation. Wide range of Welsh ales. LD3 7JD

Shopping

TALYBONT STORES - Tel: 01874 676663. Friendly and well stocked post office stores open 7am-7pm daily (8am-6pm Sun). The post office counter operates between 9am and 1.30pm Mon-Sat. LD3 7YJ

Things to Do

ASHFORD HOUSE - Tel: 01874 676271. Walled and wild gardens open to the public on Tuesday afternoons Apr-Sep under the National Gardens Scheme. Access via drive adjacent to northern portal of tunnel. Tea room and plants for sale. LD3 7YR

Connections

BUSES - service 43 as Llangynidr.

Pencelli · Map 43

Shopless village on the B4558. Down a lane to the west is Llanfigan and the isolated church of St Meugan.

Eating & Drinking

ROYAL OAK - village centre between bridges 153 and 154; visitor moorings. Tel: 01874 665396. LD3 7LX

Connections

BUSES - service 43 as Llangynidr.

Llanfrynach · Map 43

Village on the Nant Menasgin which flows off the Beacons to the Usk. Some interesting architecture.

Eating & Drinking

WHITE SWAN - village centre (half mile west of Bridge 158). Tel: 01874 665277. Picturesque country dining pub open daily (ex Tue) from 11.30am (noon on Sun). LD3 7BZ.

43 MONMOUTHSHIRE & BRECON Pencelli 4mls/0lks/2hrs

STURDY beeches clothe a sinuous cutting between bridges 146 and 147. A trio of windlass-operated lift bridges - mostly, in any case, left 'up' for the passage of boats - ensues, supplying visual variety to the prevalent stone arch structures on the rest of the canal if nothing else. Standing on a knoll across the Usk, Scethrog Tower is thought to date from the 14th century and is one of only two tower houses in Breconshire. Canallers from the North of England will acknowledge a family resemblance to their peel or pele towers. At one time it was the home of the jazz stalwart, George Melly, who purchased it so as to be able to indulge in his passion for fly fishing. Before he succumbed to lung cancer at the age of eighty in 2007, he is said to have remarked: 'I would like to die leaving the stage to the sound of applause ringing in my ears, or on the riverbank with two freshly caught trout by my side.' Incidentally, the Usk is renowned in game fishing circles for salmon and brown trout. Indeed, its Welsh name, Afon Wysg, literally translates as abundant in fish.

At Pencelli the canal is said to have incorporated the moat of one of the Marcher Lords' medieval castles. Hints of a motte & bailey fortification are apparent in the unnaturally vertiginous undergrowth, whilst a lofty farmhouse

appears to have filched a good deal of the old castle's materials in its construction.

North of Pencelli, some *deus ex machina* appears to have taken a steam iron to all the landscape's extravagantly random creases and left them neatly and more flatly folded; or at least this seems to be the case until you reach Bridge 160, where the upturned ruptures of the Brecon Beacons, dominated by Pen y Fan, remind you that this is Wales and that it is in its DNA to be wild. By bridge 158 stands a former warehouse together with an accompanying boathouse. Cambrian Cruisers' base is the northernmost on the M & B. By Peterstone Court, the canal renews its relationship with the Usk. On the offside there's evidence of an old quarry, and by a weir on the river, a converted mill.

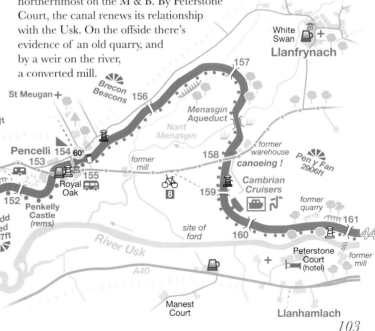

TRUE to E. F. Schumacher's tenet, 'Small is Beautiful', the Monmouthshire & Brecon Canal - all currently navigable thirty-five miles of it - approaches its northern terminus much as it has journeyed along the Usk Valley, surrounded by astonishingly lovely scenery. Tarrying on Brynich Aqueduct, beguiled by the view through the tree-tops of the Brecon Beacon's highest peak, Pen y Fan, you don't want the experience to end abruptly in Brecon; you want to break out into *Hen Wlad Fy Nhadau*; you want to be, damn it, to *be* Welsh.

Brynich Lock lifts the canal up by ten feet to its summit level of 425 feet. The trip boat, *Dragonfly*, makes regular appearances here, carrying appreciative excursionists down onto the aqueduct, bringing echoes of the Sunday School outings which were a feature of the canal in Victorian and Edwardian times. Ripples too, perhaps, of the weekly market boat which took two days to ply the canal from Newport to Brecon (42 miles and 37 locks) up until 1915, retailing domestic commodities to the isolated inhabitants of communities en route.

Nostalgically, you look back over your shoulder for one last lingering glimpse

of the Beacons before Brecon's bay windows and barracks bring you back to earth with a bump; though hopefully not into an oncoming boat. Bridge 164A carries the Brecon by-pass, the A40 being the old London to Fishguard road for the Irish ferry. The duplicated arch of Bridge 165 recalls the former Hay Railway, a tramroad which opened in 1816. Two hundred yards short of its original terminal basin, the canal performs its final act in the appropriate setting of the Theatr Brycheiniog. The present basin, created in 1997, provides as pleasant an urban mooring as you'll find anywhere on the system. One is reminded, somehow, of Ripon. Day boats are available for hire if you have absentmindedly not brought your own. But those who have will be in no hurry to turn back. The obscurity and brevity of the Mon & Brec are now revealed not as its weaknesses, but as its strengths.

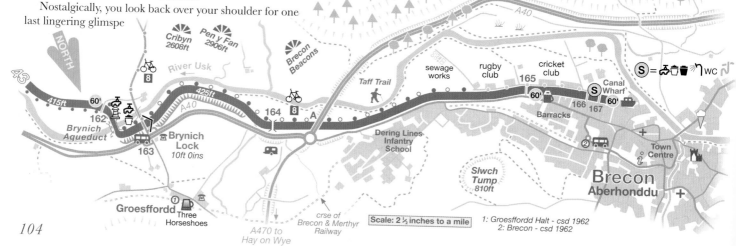

Cribyn 2608ft

Pen y Fan 2906ft

Brecon Beacons

River Usk

415ft 60'

162 60'

Brynich Aqueduct

163

Brynich Lock 10ft 0ins

Groesffordd Three Horseshoes

A470 to Hay on Wye

425ft

A40

164

A

Taff Trail

Dering Lines Infantry School

Slwch Tump 810ft

crse of Brecon & Merthyr Railway

Scale: 2½ inches to a mile

sewage works

rugby club

165

cricket club

60'

166 167

Barracks

(S) Canal Wharf 60'

(S) = WC

Brecon Aberhonddu

Town Centre

1: Groesffordd Halt - csd 1962
2: Brecon - csd 1962

NORTH

43

Brecon

Map 44

Garrison town, administrative centre for the Brecon Beacons National Park, seat of the diocese of Swansea and Brecon and mecca for walkers and climbers, Brecon is a friendly place; certainly no anti-climax at the end of a voyage up the Mon & Brec. The oldest part of town surrounds the castle remains near the confluence of the Usk and Honddu rivers. An attractive 'promenade' by the Usk, reached via Watergate, provides superb views of the Beacons. Every August, New Orleans comes to town with the staging of the internationally-renowned Brecon Jazz Festival.

Eating & Drinking

CASTLE HOTEL - Castle Square. Tel: 01874 624611. Comfortable 'country town' hotel offering bar and restaurant food to non-residents. The restaurant opens out onto a terrace with fine views over the river and distant mountains. *Good Beer Guide* listed. LD3 9DB

GURKHA CORNER - Glamorgan Street. Tel: 01874 610871. Himalayan & Nepalese cusine. LD3 7DW

THE HOURS - Ship Street. Tel: 01874 622800. Delightful cafe/bookshop opposite the library. Open Tue-Sat 10am to 5pm. Delicious breakfasts, pastries, soups, sandwiches and cakes jostle for space with a considered stock of new and secondhand books. LD3 9AD

LLANFAES DAIRY - Bridge Street (far bank of Usk). Tel: 01874 625892. Forty flavours of 'Welsh ice cream made with Italian flair'! LD3 8AH

PILGRIMS TEA ROOMS - Cathedral Close. Tel: 01874 610610. Open daily for coffees, lunches and teas with emphasis on traditional Welsh fare. LD3 9DP

THREE HORSESHOES - Groesffordd (half a mile's walk north of Brynich Lock. Tel: 01874 665672. Brecon's best eating establishment is neither in Brecon nor on the canal, yet this refurbished village pub is well worth a ten minute walk up from Brynich Lock (though do take care of the road traffic which zips by with unnerving

1 Castle Hotel
2 Gurkha Corner
3 The Hours
4 Llanfaes Dairy
5 Pilgrims Tearooms
6 Tipple 'N' Tiffin

velocity. The bar features a good range of local ales and functions convivially as 'a local'. The restaurant offers stunning views of Pen Y Fan and serves food to match. *Good Beer Guide* listed. LD3 7SN

TIPPLE 'N' TIFFIN - Canal Wharf. Tel: 01874 611866. Informal 'theatre' dining at canal basin, open daily (ex Sun) 10am-3pm and 7pm to 10pm. LD3 7EW

Shopping

Most of the major stores you'd expect to find in a town of this size, many of them in the Bethel Square shopping precinct by the main car park. Plenty of outdoor activity shops - a good place to buy that new pair of walking boots you've been promising yourself. The charming indoor market dates from 1840 and markets are held on Tuesdays and Fridays with the addition of farmer's markets on the second Saturday of each month. Morrisons, Co-op (PO) and Aldi supermarkets. Andrew Morton's on Lion Yard is a good outlet for secondhand books. Beacon's Laundry on St Mary's Street will refresh your best boating attire.

Things to Do

TOURIST INFORMATION CENTRE - Cattle Market Car Park. Tel: 01874 622485. LD3 9DA

BEACON PARK DAY BOATS - Canal Basin. Tel: 0800 612 2890. Electric day boat and canoe hire. LD3 7FD

BIKES & HIKES - Lion Yard. Tel: 01874 610071. Bicycle sales, servicing and hire. Canoes also. LD3 7BA

BIPED CYCLES - Ship Street. Tel: 01874 622296. Bike sales, service and hire. LD3 9AF

BRECKNOCK MUSEUM - Captain's Walk. Closed pending refurbishment as Cultural Hub. LD3 7DS

BRECON BOATHOUSE - The Promenade. Tel: 01874 622995. Pedalos and rowing boats for hire on the Usk. LD3 9AY

BRECON CATHEDRAL - Tel: 01874 625222. Former Benedictine priory refurbished by George Gilbert Scott in 1872. Tithe barn heritage centre and restaurant. LD3 9DP

DRAGONFLY CRUISES - Canal Wharf. Tel: 0783 168 5222. Public boat trips from Brecon out to Brynich Lock and back. Also: Picnic Boat hire. LD3 7EW

REGIMENTAL MUSEUM - The Barracks. Tel: 01874 613310. Open weekdays 10am-5pm, plus Saturdays Apr-Sep and Sundays in August. Features the exploits of the South Wales Borderers at Rorke's Drift in the Zulu War of 1879 when 140 soldiers stood firm against four thousand Zulu warriors. LD3 7PY

THEATR BRYCHEINIOG - Canal Wharf. Tel: 01874 611622. Performing arts venue. LD3 7EW

Connections

BUSES - services X43/43 run Mon-Sat to/from Abergavenny via Crickhowell, the former sticking to the A40, the latter serving canalside villages. Service 39 links Brecon with Hereford via the famous bookselling town of Hay. T4 runs to/from Cardiff via Merthyr Tydfil and Pontypridd. Tel: 0871 200 2233.

TAXIS - Brecon Taxis Tel: 01874 623444.

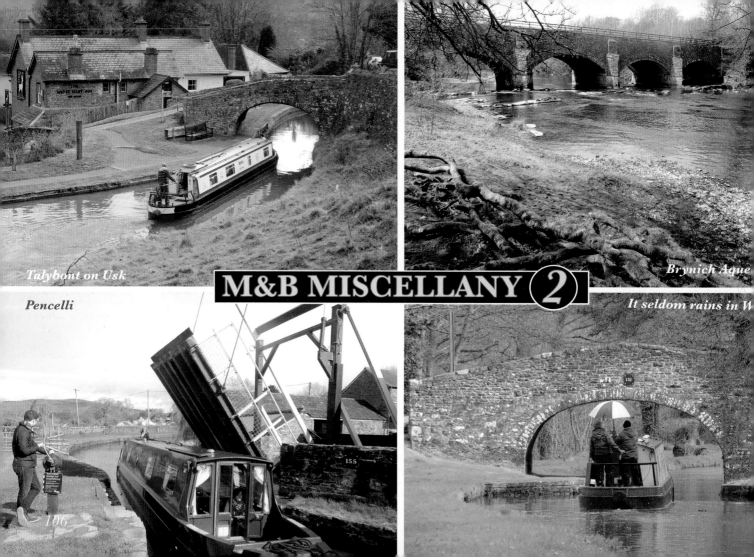

Talybont on Usk

Brynich Aque

Pencelli

It seldom rains in W

M&B MISCELLANY ②

106

This Guide

Pearson's Canal Companions are a long established, independently produced series of guide books devoted to the inland waterways and designed to appeal equally to boaters, walkers, cyclists and other, less readily pigeon-holed members of society. Considerable pride is taken to make these guides as up to date, accurate, entertaining and inspirational as possible. A good guide book should fulfil three functions: make you want to go; interpret the lie of the land when you're there; and provide a lasting souvenir of your journeys. It is to be hoped that this guide ticks all three boxes, and possibly more besides.

The Maps

There are forty-six numbered maps whose layout is shown by the Route Planner inside the front cover. Maps 1 to 16 cover the 'main line' of the Shropshire Union Canal between Autherley Junction (Wolverhampton) and Ellesmere Port; Maps 11A & 11B cover the Middlewich Branch between Barbridge and Middlewich; Maps 17 to 26 cover the Llangollen Canal from Hurleston Junction (Nantwich) to Horseshoe Falls (Llangollen); Maps 27 to 34 cover the Montgomery Canal from Frankton to Newtown (users should note that this canal is only partially navigable at present); Maps 35 to 44 cover the Monmouthshire & Brecon Canal from Pontnewydd (Cwmbran) to Brecon.

The maps - measured imperially like the waterways they depict, and not being slavishly north-facing - are easily read in either direction. Users will thus find most itineraries progressing smoothly and logically from left to right or vice versa. Figures quoted at the top of each map refer to distance per map, locks per map and average cruising time.

INFORMATION

An alternative indication of timings from centre to centre can be found on the Route Planner. Obviously, cruising times vary with the nature of your boat and the number of crew at your disposal, so quoted times should be taken only as an estimate. Neither do times quoted take into account any delays which might occur at lock flights in high season. Walking and cycling times will depend very much on the state of individual sections of towpath and stamina.

The Text

Each map is accompanied by a route commentary placing the waterway in its historic, social and topographical context. As close to each map as is feasible, gazetteer-like entries are given for places passed through, listing, where appropriate, facilities of significance to users of this guide. Every effort is made to ensure these details are as up to date as possible, but - especially where pubs/restaurants are concerned - we suggest you telephone ahead if relying upon an entry to provide you with a meal at any given time.

Walking

The simplest way to explore the inland waterways is on foot along towpaths originally provided so that horses could 'tow' boats. Walking costs little more than the price of shoe leather and you are free to concentrate on the passing scene; something that boaters, with the responsibilities of navigation thrust upon them, are not always at liberty to do. The maps set out to give some idea of the quality of the towpath on any given section of canal. More of an art than a science to be sure, but at least it reflects our personal experiences, and whilst it does vary from area to area, none of it should prove problematical for anyone inured to the vicissitudes of country walking.

We recommend the use of public transport to facilitate 'one-way' itineraries but stress the advisability of checking up to date details on the telephone numbers quoted, or on the websites of National Rail Enquiries or Traveline for trains and buses respectively.

As reliable as we trust this guide will be, the additional use of an up to date Ordnance Survey Landranger or Explorer sheet is recommended as they are able to present your chosen route in a broader context. Should you be considering walking the full length of these paths over several consecutive days, Tourist Information Centres can usually be relied upon to offer accommodation advice.

Cycling

Bicycling along towpaths is an increasingly popular pastime, though one not always equally popular with other waterway users such as boaters, anglers and pedestrians. It is important to remember that you are sharing the towpath with other people out for their own form of enjoyment, and to treat them with the respect and politeness they deserve. A bell is a useful form of diplomacy; failing that, a stentorian cough. Happily, since the inception of the Canal & River Trust, it is no longer necessary for cyclists to acquire a permit to use the towpath.

Boating

Boating on inland waterways is an established, though relatively small, facet of the UK tourist industry. It is also, increasingly, a chosen lifestyle. There are approximately 35,000 privately owned boats registered on the inland waterways, but in addition to these, numerous firms offer boats for hire. These range from small operators with half a dozen boats to sizeable fleets run by companies with several bases.

Most hire craft have all the creature comforts you are likely to expect. In the excitement of planning a boating holiday you may give scant thought to the contents of your hire boat, but at the end of a hard day's boating such matters take on more significance, and a well equipped, comfortable boat, large enough to accommodate your crew with something to spare, can make the difference between a good holiday and one which will be shudderingly remembered for the

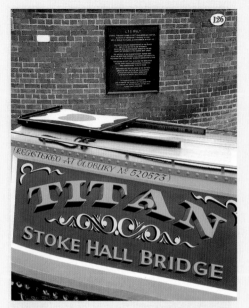

wrong reasons.

Traditionally, hire boats are booked out by the week or fortnight, though many firms now offer more flexible short breaks or extended weeks. All reputable hire firms give newcomers tuition in boat handling and lock working, and first-timers soon find themselves adapting to the pace of things 'on the cut'.

Navigational Advice

Newcomers, hiring a boat on the inland waterways for the first time, have every right to expect sympathetic and thorough tuition from the company providing their boat. Boat-owners are, by definition, likely to be already adept at navigating. The following, however, may prove useful points of reference.

Locks are part of the charm of inland waterway cruising, but they can be potentially dangerous environments for children, pets and careless adults. Use of them should be methodical and unhurried, whilst special care should be exercised in rain, frost and snow when slippery hazards abound.

The majority of locks included in this guide are of the narrow variety. However, on the Shropshire Union Canal north of Nantwich they are widebeam and capable of accommodating two narrowboats side by side. There are 'staircase' locks at Bunbury, Chester Northgate, Grindley Brook and Frankton where adjacent chambers share common gates. When working uphill the upper chamber must be full so that the water in it can be released to fill the lower chamber. Going downhill, the lower chamber must be empty to enable the water from the upper chamber to flow into it.

Finally, it behoves us all to be on our best behaviour at locks. Remember to exercise a little 'give and take'. The use of foul mouths or fists to decide precedence at locks is one canal tradition not worthy of preservation.

Lift Bridges are a feature of the Llangollen, Montgomery and Monmouthshire & Brecon canals. Great care should be taken to ensure that the bridge platform remains firmly upright as your boat passes through. Most lift bridges are manually operated employing a windlass, though a couple on the little used Welshpool section of the Montgomery Canal still rely on the time-honoured method of pulling down on a chain. The lift bridges at Wrenbury (Llangollen Canal) and Talybont (Mon & Brec) are electrically operated using a Canal & River Trust Yale key.

Mooring on the canals featured in this guide is per usual practice - ie on the towpath side, away from sharp bends, bridge-holes and narrows. An open, yellow-tinted bollard symbol represents visitor mooring sites; either as designated specifically by the Canal & River Trust and the Shropshire Union Canal Society or, in some cases, as suggested by our personal experience.

Turning points on the canals are known as 'winding holes'; pronounced as the thing which blows because in the old days the wind was expected to do much of the work rather than the boatman. It is advisable to go in bow first. Winding holes capable of taking a full length boat of around seventy foot length are marked where appropriate on the maps. Winding holes capable of turning shorter craft are marked with the approximate length. It is of course possible to turn boats at junctions and at most boatyards, though in the case of the latter it is considered polite to seek permission before doing so.

Boating facilities are provided at regular intervals along the inland waterways, and range from a simple water tap or refuse disposal skip, to the provision of sewage disposal, showers and laundry. Such vital features are also obtainable at boatyards and marinas along with repairs and servicing. An alphabetical list of boatyards appears overleaf on pages 110 & 111.

Closures (or 'stoppages' in canal parlance) traditionally occur on the inland waterways between November and April, during which time most of the heavy maintenance work is undertaken. Occasionally, however, an emergency stoppage, or perhaps water restriction, may be imposed at short notice, closing part of the route you intend to use.

Private Navigations which connect with Canal & River Trust canals covered in this guide are the Manchester Ship Canal at Ellesmere Port (Map 16) and the River Dee at Chester (Map 15). Hire boaters will not be permitted to enter either of these waterways; private pleasure craft may use the MSC only if they comply with a number of strict conditions, such as Third Party insurance and a Certificate of Seaworthiness. A downloadable pdf is available from the ship canal's owners www.peelports.com. Or contact the Harbour Master, Queen Elizabeth II Dock, Eastham, Wirral CH62 0BB. Tel: 0151 327 1461.

The Dee below Chester is a tidal, fast flowing river not recommended for use by canal craft. The Upper Dee, however, flows charmingly through the Cheshire countryside and may (or may not!) be reached by prior arrangement with CRT - Tel: 0303 040 4040) via the Dee Branch. To boat the Dee one must additionally contact Chester City Council, The Forum, Chester CH1 2HS. Tel: 0300 123 8123.

Useful Contacts
Canal & River Trust
First Floor North, Station House, 500 Elder Gate Milton Keynes MK9 1BB Tel: 0303 040 4040 *www.canalrivertrust.org.uk*

The routes contained in this guide are looked after from regional offices in Northwich and Gloucester.

Societies
The Inland Waterways Association was founded in 1946 to campaign for the retention of the canal system. Many routes now open to pleasure boaters may not have been so but for this organisation. Membership details, together with details of the IWA's regional branches, may be obtained from: Inland Waterways Association, Island House, Moor Road, Chesham HP5 1WA. Tel: 01494 783453. *www.waterways.org.uk*

The Shropshire Union Canal Society take a keen interest in the canals of the old Shropshire Union system: *www.shropshireunion.org.uk*

The Monmouthshire, Brecon & Abergavenny Canals Trust are campaigning for restoration of further lengths of their canal. *www.mbact.org.uk*

The Chester Canal Heritage Trust's activities can be appreciated on *www.chestercanalheritagetrust.co.uk*

Acknowledgements
The Canal Companions are nurtured - one might go as far as saying 'lovingly' - by a small team of perfectionists too self-effacing to require the oxygen of publicity. Suffice it to say that the publishers are enormously grateful for all their efforts, but that anonymity would be inappropriate where the inestimable Karen Tanguy, Meg (signwriter *extraordinaire*) Gregory, and Hawksworth, surpassing printers of Uttoxeter are concerned. Ditto Jackie P. who went reluctantly boating, not just once but *twice!*

Hire Bases

ABC BOAT HIRE - Ellesmere, Llangollen Canal, Map 22. Tel: 0330 333 0590.
www.abcboathire.com SY12 9DD

ABC BOAT HIRE - Goytre Wharf, Monmouthshire & Brecon Canal, Map 37. Tel: 0330 333 0590.
www.abcboathire.com NP7 9EW

ABC BOAT HIRE - Whitchurch, Llangollen Canal, Map 19. Tel: 0330 333 0590.
www.abcboathire.com SY13 3AA

ABC BOAT HIRE - Wrenbury, Llangollen Canal, Map 18. Tel: 0330 333 0590.
www.abcboathire.com CW5 8HG

ANDERSEN BOATS - Middlewich, Trent & Mersey Canal, Map 11B. Tel: 01606 833668.
www.andersenboats.com CW10 9BQ

ANGLO WELSH - Bunbury, Shropshire Union Canal, Map 12. Tel: 0117 304 1122.
www.anglowelsh.co.uk CW6 9QB

ANGLO WELSH - Trevor, Llangollen Canal, Map 25. Tel: 0117 304 1122. *www.anglowelsh.co.uk* LL20 7TX

BEACON PARK BOATS - Llangattock, Monmouthshire & Brecon Canal, Map 40. Tel: 01873 858277. *www.beaconparkboats.com* NP8 1EQ

BETTISFIELD BOATS - Bettisfield, Llangollen Canal, Map 21. Tel: 01948 710494.
www.bettisfieldboats.com SY13 2LJ

BLACK PRINCE NARROWBOATS - Chirk, Llangollen Canal, Map 25. Tel: 01527 575115.
www.black-prince.com LL14 5AD

CAMBRIAN CRUISERS - Pencelli, Monmouthshire & Brecon Canal, Map 43. Tel: 01874 665315.
www.cambriancruisers.co.uk LD3 7LJ

CASTLE NARROWBOATS - Gilwern, Monmouthshire & Brecon Canal, Map 39. Tel: 01873 830001. *www.castlenarrowboats.co.uk* NP7 0EP

CHESHIRE CAT - Overwater Marina, Shropshire Union Canal, Map 9. Tel: 0786 779 0195.
www.cheshirecatnarrowboats.co.uk CW5 8AY

COUNTRY CRAFT - Llangynidr, Monmouthshire & Brecon Canal, Map 42. Tel: 01874 730850.
www.country-craft.co.uk NP8 1ND

COUNTRYWIDE CRUISERS - Brewood, Shropshire Union Canal, Map 2. Tel: 01902 850166.
www.countrywide-cruisers.com ST19 9BG

CREST NARROWBOATS - Chirk, Llangollen Canal, Map 25. Tel: 01691 774558.
www.crestnarrowboats.co.uk LL14 5AD

CHAS HARDERN - Beeston, Shropshire Union Canal, Map 12. Tel: 01829 732595.
www.chashardern.co.uk CW6 9NH

HIRE A CANAL BOAT - Whixall & Chirk, Llangollen Canal, Maps 21 & 25. Tel: 01395 443529.
www.hireacanalboat.co.uk SY13 2QS/LL14 5AD

MARINE CRUISES - Swanley Bridge, Llangollen Canal, Map 17. Tel: 01244 373911.
www.marinecruises.co.uk CW5 8NR

MAESTERMYN HIRE CRUISERS* - Whittington, Llangollen Canal, Map 23. Tel: 01691 662424.
www.maestermyn.co.uk SY11 4NU

MIDDLEWICH NARROWBOATS - Middlewich, Trent & Mersey Canal, Map 11B. Tel: 01606 832460.
www.middlewichboats.co.uk CW10 9BD

NAPTON NARROWBOATS - Autherley Junction, Shropshire Union Canal, Map 1. Tel: 01926 813644.
www.napton-marina.co.uk WV9 5HW

NORBURY WHARF - Norbury Junction, Shropshire Union Canal, Map 5. Tel: 01785 284292.
www.norburyhire.co.uk ST20 0PN

PEA GREEN BOATS - Whixall Marina, Llangollen Canal, Map 21. Tel: 0757 006 8561.
www.peagreenboats.co.uk SY13 2QS

ROAD HOUSE HIRE - Gilwern, Monmouthshire & Brecon Canal, Map 39. Tel: 01873 830240.
www.narrowboats-wales.co.uk NP7 0AS

VENETIAN - Venetian Marina, Middlewich Arm, Map 11A. Tel: 01270 528122
www.venetianhireboats.co.uk CW5 6DD

* AKA Mid Wales Narrowboats & Welsh Lady

Day Boat Hire

BEACON PARK DAY BOATS - Brecon, Mon & Brec Canal, Map 44. Tel: 0796 646 1819. LD3 7FD

BLACKWATER MEADOW MARINA (ABC) - Ellesmere, Llangollen Canal, Map 22. Tel: 01691 624391. SY12 9DD

DRAGONFLY DAY BOATS - Brecon, Mon & Brec Canal, Map 44. Tel: 0771 225 3432. LD3 7EW

GOYTRE WHARF MARINA (ABC) - Llanover, Monmouthshire & Brecon Canal, Map 41. Tel: 01873 880516. NP7 9EW

MIDWAY BOATS - Barbridge, Shropshire Union Canal, Map 11. Tel: 01270 528482. CW5 6BE

NANTWICH MARINA - Nantwich, Shropshire Union Canal, Map 11. Tel: 01270 625122. CW5 8LB

NORBURY WHARF - Norbury Junction, Shropshire Union, Map 5. Tel: 01785 284292. ST20 0PN

WHITCHURCH MARINA (ABC) - Whitchurch, Llangollen Canal, Map 19. Tel: 01948 662012. SY13 3AA

Boatyards

ANGLO WELSH - Bunbury, Shropshire Union Canal, Map 12. Tel: 01829 260957. CW6 9QB

ANGLO WELSH - Trevor, Llangollen Canal, Map 25. Tel: 01978 821749. LL20 7TX

AQUEDUCT MARINA - Church Minshull, Middlewich Branch, Map 11A. Tel: 01270 525040. CW5 6DX

BARBRIDGE MARINA/MIDWAY BOATS - Barbridge, Shropshire Union Canal, Map 11. Tel: 01270 528482. CW5 6BE

BLACKWATER MEADOW MARINA (ABC) - Ellesmere, Llangollen Canal, Map 22. Tel: 01691 624391. SY12 9DD

CAMBRIAN CRUISERS - Pencelli, Mon & Brecon Canal, Map 43. Tel: 01874 665315. LD3 7LJ

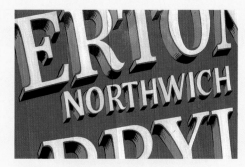

CASTLE NARROWBOATS - Gilwern, Monmouthshire & Brecon Canal, Map 39. Tel: 01873 830001. NP7 0EP

CHIRK MARINA - Chirk, Llangollen Canal, Map 25. Tel: 01691 774558. LL14 5AD

COUNTRY CRAFT - Llangynidr, Monmouthshire & Brecon Canal, Map 42. Tel: 01874 730850. NP8 1ND

COUNTRYWIDE CRUISERS - Brewood, Shropshire Union Canal, Map 2. Tel: 01902 850166. ST19 9BG

GOYTRE WHARF MARINA (ABC) - Llanover, Monmouthshire & Brecon Canal, Map 37. Tel: 01873 880516. NP7 9EW

CHAS HARDERN - Beeston, Shropshire Union Canal, Map 12. Tel: 01829 732595. CW6 9NH

HERON'S REST MARINA - Llangattock, Monmouthshire & Brecon Canal, Map 40. Tel: 01873 810223. NP8 1HS

KING'S LOCK CHANDLERY - Middlewich, Trent & Mersey Canal, Map 11B. Tel: 01606 737564. CW10 0JJ

MAESTERMYN MARINE - Whittington, Llangollen Canal, Map 23. Tel: 01691 662424. SY11 4NU

NANTWICH MARINA - Nantwich, Shropshire Union Canal, Map 11. Tel: 01270 625122. CW5 8LB

NAPTON NARROWBOATS (AUTHERLEY) - Autherley Junction, Shropshire Union Canal, Map 1. Tel: 01902 789942. WV9 5HW

NORBURY WHARF - Norbury Junction, Shropshire Union Canal, Map 5. Tel: 01785 284292. ST20 0PN

OXLEY MARINE - Autherley, Staffs & Worcs Canal, Map 1. Tel: 01902 789522. WV10 6TZ

OVERWATER MARINA - Audlem, Shropshire Union Canal, Map 9. Tel: 01270 812677. CW5 8AY

ROAD HOUSE NARROWBOATS - Gilwern, Monmouthshire & Brecon Canal, Map 39. Tel: 01873 830240. NP7 0AS

SWANLEY BRIDGE MARINA - Swanley, Llangollen Canal, Map 17. Tel: 01270 524571. CW5 8NR

TALBOT WHARF - Market Drayton, Shropshire Union Canal, Map 8. Tel: 01630 652641. TF9 1HN

TAYLOR'S BOATYARD - Chester, Shropshire Union Canal, Map 15. Tel: 01244 379922. CH1 4FB

TATTENHALL MARINA - Tattenhall, Shropshire Union Canal, Map 13. Tel: 01829 771742. CH3 9NE

VENETIAN MARINA - Cholmondeston, Shropshire Union Canal Middlewich Branch, Map 11A. Tel: 01270 52878. CW5 6DD

WHITCHURCH MARINA (ABC) - Whitchurch, Llangollen Canal, Map 19. Tel: 01948 662012. SY13 3AA

WHIXALL MARINA (BWML) - Whixall, Llangollen Canal, Map 21. Tel: 01948 880420. SY13 2QS

WRENBURY MILL MARINA (ABC) - Wrenbury, Llangollen Canal, Map 18. Tel: 01270 780544. CW5 8HG

Nine More Reasons for Exploring the Canals with Pearsons

9th edition - ISBN 978 0 9562777 4 9

10th edition - ISBN 978 0 9562777 8 7

8th edition - ISBN 978 0 9562777 2 5

1st edition - ISBN 978 0 9928492 1 4

7th edition - ISBN 978 0 9562777 5 6

9th edition - ISBN 978 0 9562777 3 2

8th edition - ISBN 978 0 9562777 9 4

1st edition - ISBN 978 0 9928492 0 7

3rd edition - ISBN 978 0 9562777 6 3

Pearson's Canal Companions are published by Wayzgoose. They are widely available from hire bases, boatyards, canal shops, good bookshops, via Amazon and other internet outlets.